CROSS
CANADA
COOKING

FAVORITE RECIPES OF CANADIANS FROM MANY LANDS

Hancock House Publishers Ltd.

Canada Cooking

by SONDRA GOTLIEB

ISBN 0-919654-52-5

This book was designed and first produced in
Canada by Hancock House Publishers Limited
3215 Island View Road, Saanichton, British
Columbia, Canada.

Designed by Nicholas Newbeck Design
Typesetting by Monday Magazine
Printed by D.W. Friesen & Sons Limited,
Altona, Manitoba

Printed in Canada

Canadian Shared Cataloguing in Publication Data
Gotlieb, Sondra, 1936-
    Cross Canada Cooking
    "IC cat. no. S96-2/1976
    Includes index
    ISBN 0-919654-52-5

    1. Cookery, Canadian 2. Cookery,
    International. I. Title.
    TX715.G68   641.5   C76-016017-1

HANCOCK HOUSE PUBLISHERS LTD.
3215 Island View Road
Saanichton, British Columbia, Canada

Portions of this book have appeared earlier in the
author's THE GOURMET'S CANADA,
published by New Press, Toronto, and in
CHATELAINE magazine.

Contents

Introduction

When I started writing this book I was stymied. My purpose was to write something on the ethnic and regional gastronomic customs in Canada. But everyone knows that oatmeal means Scotch, spaghetti means Italian, and gefilte fish, Jewish. There were recipe books to prove it. I certainly didn't want to write in a vaguely general way what I thought the Lunenburgers were supposed to be cooking in Nova Scotia, or what the Eastern-European immigrants who settled in North Winnipeg might have cooked at the turn of the century. And I was well aware that everyone in Canada, whether new Chinese settlers, six months out of Hong Kong, or descendants of the Family Compact ate steak, hamburgers and Kentucky Fried. I needed personal contact; I wanted to find out if there were people who cooked in a manner that bore some relationship to their ancestry or region. I wanted to find out who they were, how they lived, and what the food they cooked in their own kitchens tasted like. Eating well is a satisfying human experience, and I needed human beings to bring this book to life. I was terribly lucky. People I had never met before from all the strata of Canadian society, fishermens' wives, businessmen, tailors' and doctors' families invited me into their kitchens and dining rooms to see how they cooked codfish or chicken tika, lasagne or plum dumplings. They prepared the most elaborate meals for a total stranger, because they were proud of their cooking tradition and wished to see it preserved in print.

The common links between all the groups, whether Ugandan Indian or Irish Newfoundland, were warmth, hospitality and good food. I was also surprised to find a specific gastronomic link between every culture I visited — the tradition of wrapping dough around meat, vegetables and fruit. This is, of course, a practical and delicious way of making food go further and using up leftovers to their best advantage. Canadians from every culture come from thrifty stock. Starting east, in Newfoundland, we have salt pork buns, on to Nova Scotia for apple dumplings, on to New Brunswick Acadians for poutine à trou, and then to Quebec for tourtière. Multicultured Ontario has plum dumplings, palatschinken and tortellini (from the Austro-Hungarian Empire and Italy). North Winnipeg and the western provinces have Jewish blintzes, Mennonite piroschki, Ukrainian pyrohy, Greek pites, and Icelandic pönnukökur; Vancouver (as well as central Canada) has large Chinese, Japanese and East Indian cultures that make won ton, tempura and pakoras. Soft or crisp, dough or batter, with or without yeast, all are envelopes containing something else. I left out some of these recipes because I was afraid — even though there were great variations — that the theme had been sufficiently played.

"Old Canadian" descendants of founding settlers like André Ouellette from Montreal, and Jean Boyd from Halifax, still hankered after tourtière and oatcakes, respectively. Both have made the other's traditional food as well as Greek, Chinese, and Italian recipes, but their pride in maintaining their distinctive cooking styles was gratifying. It was interesting talking to Joan Wong who adapts Chinese recipes to Canadian ingredients. She greeted me with "I buy everything at Loblaws." And if Loblaws doesn't have all the ingredients, there is sure to be a grocery store that didn't exist in Canada twenty years ago, selling vine leaves for Mrs. Cholakis' dolmathes, or coconut paste for Bhagwant Natt's curry. The increase of cooking styles and ingredients in the country can only help to broaden and enrich everyone. Young people, with not a drop of Chinese, Italian, or Hungarian blood in them, shop for dried mushrooms, black olives and paprika sausage at the Kensington Market in Toronto, and groceries and delicatessens in all the provinces.

8

It was impossible for me to visit someone from every region and ethnic group in Canada. This book is just a sampling of the kinds of cooking that take place in some people's homes. Time, lack of opportunity, and a growing realization that my task would become encyclopedic and unending if I pursued every ethnic group in Canada, placed limits on me.

I have tried to do justice to what I considered the most interesting cooking styles among the varied backgrounds of Canadians, as well as describing the cooking traditions of families from the major cultures in Canada. The eastern Europeans, the Germans (in the form of the old Lunenburg settlers, and the Ontario Mennonites), the Italians, are some of the largest groups with distinct cooking styles, and I've included our founding settlers, the Scotch, the French Canadians, the Acadians. Other groups like the Chinese and Japanese have made a great contribution to the culinary habits of Canada and cannot be ignored. And Newfoundland is in a class by itself. It is the only province outside of Quebec that has an identifiable and unusual style of cooking that is still thriving.

My own sentiment, memories and prejudices account for the rest of the people in this book. The Icelanders, though a relatively small group, played a great role in settling Manitoba, and as a child I adored the school teas, because I could grab a piece of vinaterta off a tray, if the teachers were not looking. I could not write about Jewish cooking from an objective point of view. My own experiences growing up in Winnipeg had to be exposed.

This book is not an encyclopedia of multicultural recipes; it is an account of what people like you and me are cooking in their kitchens now.

About the Recipes

You might notice that I have not given the recipe for every dish I tasted. And I have added recipes of my own choice that I developed from various regional and ethnic cookbooks. My book gives a sampling of dishes from fifteen different cultures. I felt that some very complicated recipes, like Mrs. Di Cecco's tortellini, Mrs. Vlassie's phyllo dough, Mrs. Birnbaum's wedding strudel, would require a textbook on their handling, as well as forty years experience. My aim is to offer recipes that are within the realm of possibility of a willing amateur. Doughs that need stretching, pulling, drying and careful cutting are for professionals like the ladies I have just mentioned. The recipes I have included seemed interesting and fairly easy to reproduce. All the recipes in the book have been personally tested. But the the people who kindly gave me their recipes are, generally speaking, a pinch of this and a handful of that kind of cooks. Few follow exact measurements; they find that it cramps their style and inspiration to worry about how much flour, or how many shrimps, go into a dish. If I could not duplicate what I ate in their houses, in my house, I left the recipe out. I also left out some because I did not like them. Sheer personal prejudice.

Most items in the recipes can be bought at supermarkets, Indian, Chinese, or Japanese or Italian groceries, which as I mentioned are becoming more and more plentiful.

1. Seal Flippers & Corned Caplin

Emmy Lou and John Allan own a pleasant ranch style house in the center of St. John's, Newfoundland; John is a salesman and Emmy Lou looks far too young to have a daughter in nursing. The only difference between them and thousands of other Canadians who go to Florida for a winter vacation is that John packs corned caplin and dried pea beans in his golf bag. Corned caplin, (a kind of smelt), are dried and salted bits of silvery leathery fish. Newfoundlanders like them better than pretzels with their beer or rum and coke. The pea beans are for pease pudding. Where can you get pease pudding around Tampa? Emmy Lou boils them up in a cheesecloth bag, and serves them with salt ribs for a "Jiggs" or boiled dinner. When Newfoundlanders emigrate to the rest of Canada they suffer withdrawal symptoms because of the deprivation of salt ribs and other beloved foods. In response to this condition, small but thriving shops owned by someone from Heart's Desire or Famish (from famished) Gut, Newfoundland, have opened in many Canadian cities, and stock salt ribs in barrels of brine, "hard bread" or biscuits, made by the Purity Company, cans of turnip tops, cod and caplin, salted and dried. (The hard bread is for soaking overnight and then it's fried and eaten with salt cod, a Newfoundland specialty called fish and brewis.)

Besides salt ribs and cod and caplin, Newfoundlanders are fond of the flesh of a mammal that lives right off their Labrador coast. Seal flipper pie is a delicacy, peculiar to this province, and every year Emmy Lou Allan buys fresh seal flippers and sets aside a day or so to make her pies. She says it's vital to scrape away the hair and cut off all the blubber; otherwise flipper can be sickening. She simmers the flippers for a long time, cracks their knuckles and renders and scrapes some more. After adding savory, fat back pork and flour to the flippers, and then more cooking, she puts the stew-like mixture in foil containers, covers them with pastry and freezes the pies. All you have to do is find a seal flipper. But remember, after you eat the pie, your pores will exude seal oil for seven days. With all that vitamin D in your system, you'll never catch a cold.

When I arrived in St. John's, I had heard of flipper pie but was skeptical about finding someone who actually makes it. Emmy Lou and John asked me for dinner, with their friends, Frank and Sonya Ryan; that evening I discovered that flipper pie tastes a little like old goose but retains the smell of the windy Labrador Coast. I ask forgiveness from all Newfoundlanders, especially Emmy Lou and John. My mainland tastebuds, corroded by garlic, chili peppers, hormone fed domestic birds, couldn't decide whether seal flipper was fish or fowl, and retreated in confusion. The rum, however, (sailor's milk in the Atlantic provinces), the butter tarts, and trifle were perfect and touched base on Newfoundland's English-Irish heritage.

What's so special about Newfoundland? I hear this question over and over from curious mainlanders who wonder why tourists fuss over such a stony land, with hardly a warm bay to swim in, even in the middle of summer. Solitude, hard times, rough climate, along with misery, produce self-reliance and conservative values, and appreciation for the old ways that have given Newfoundland a unique, unmistakable flavor.

Although Ontario, for example, was heavily settled by English and Irish much later than Newfoundland, American customs across the border transformed Ontario's Anglo-Celt heritage. But Newfoundlanders, because of their geographic isolation, remained relatively untouched for a very long time by American or even Canadian mainland influences. Philologists claim that the Newfoundland accent and vocabulary, especially from the more remote outports, resemble those of English and Irish seamen of three hundred years ago. The same might be said for Newfoundland's culinary customs. Local recipe books, published by small church and community groups, are filled with contributions from women born in outports like Topsail, Seldom Come By and Joe Batts Arm. These fishermen's wives give their favorite version of Pease Pudding or Figged Duff (a raisin and

12

molasses pudding) and set down ingredients like salt cod or fish and "hard bread" (hard tack biscuits) for brewis — all favorite and essential foods of English and Irish seamen many centuries ago.

Newfoundland owes its existence to cod. Dried cod has been the staple food of Europe's peasantry since medieval times. In 1900, when Joey Smallwood was a boy, three-quarters of Newfoundland's population were either fishing, drying, salting, or shipping cod, to Spain, Portugal and France. It does not come as a shock to learn that a classic Newfoundland outport meal is salt fish. (The word 'fish' in the phrase "salt fish" always means cod. Fish in Newfoundland is cod, and if you want a bit of smoked haddock, better specify.)

Josephine Davis is the daughter of a fisherman from St. Mary's Bay, and her husband is a fisheries officer who boards Russian vessels (among other duties) to make sure their catch of cod or caplin does not exceed Canadian law. A slim pretty woman in her thirties, Josephine lives with her husband and four children in Colinet, one of Newfoundland's outports. Besides doing all her own housework, including baking the family's supply of bread, she teaches at Our Lady of Mount Carmel High School, and during the "idle" summer months and winter evenings, takes University credits in psychology, physical education and the care of the physically handicapped.

I was staying with Mary Pratt, the artist, at St. Mary's Bay, when Josephine, despite all the demands on her time, volunteered to come over and make a typical salt fish dinner. "Salt fish, with turnips and potatoes and blueberry pudding for dessert. Nothing fancy," she warned, "just what I feed my family."

When Josephine arrived she had already soaked the cod overnight, and then, at Mary's place, boiled it for twenty-five minutes, strained out the water, in case it had become oversalted, and simmered the fish in fresh water for another ten minutes. With the fish, Josephine prepared a drawn, or as some Newfoundlanders say, a "drying" butter sauce, an unctuous mixture of butter, flour, water and onions. Josephine, Mary and I ate the sauced salt fish, with boiled turnips and potatoes; root vegetables are the classic accompaniment to this

13

Maritime dish; their blander flavor harmonizes perfectly with the tender salt cod.

The year before, Josephine had frozen some blueberries (which she had picked) without sugar, in a plastic container. As she stirred them in the pudding batter, she offered her opinion on the other classical Newfoundland dish I had eaten. "It's not every Newfoundlander, you know, who likes flipper pie."

Earlier in the week, Mary took me for lunch to her mother-in-law, Mrs. Christine Pratt, who lives in a house, high up on a cliff facing the sea, just outside of St. John's. Mary's husband is artist Christopher Pratt, and his parents' house is filled with both Mary's and Christopher's impeccably drawn but haunting pictures. Mrs. Pratt is a descendant of the Dawes family, who have been living in Newfoundland since the sixteenth century. She and her sister, Aunt Myrt, an endearingly small, round lady who always wears no-nonsense but well-cut gray slacks, gave us fish chowder, Newfoundland crab on toast, and partridgeberry pudding smothered with Mrs. Pratt's special egg sauce. While Mary and I demolished everything, they told us stories about the fights between the Liberals and Conservatives, and Catholics and Protestants, that are as much a part of Newfoundland's heritage as partridgeberry pudding. Partridgeberries look like blueberries, but are deep red in color. Some people call them lingonberries, like the Scandinavians who import them from Newfoundland, where they grow wild.

Here's Mrs. Pratt's recipe for egg sauce and partridgeberry pudding. It's not difficult to make. Naturally you can substitute blueberries or cranberries for the partridgeberries.

Partridgeberry Pudding

Cream butter with sugar, add eggs, sift flour with baking powder and salt, add flour alternately with milk. Mix in berries last. Bake about ½ hour.

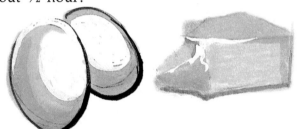

Preheat oven to 350 ° F [175 ° C]

½ cup butter or shortening
   a scant cup sugar
2 eggs
2 cups flour
2 heaping tsp. baking powder
½ tsp. salt
½ cup milk
10 oz. pkg. berries or 1 or 2 cups [280g]

Mrs. Pratt's Egg Sauce

(Use a double boiler.) Beat eggs. Melt sugar and butter together. Add eggs and keep stirring until thickened, slightly. It takes about 10 minutes. May be kept over warm water for several hours.

¾ cup butter
1 cup sugar
2 eggs

Newfoundlanders like homemade bread. Everywhere I went, I heard heated discussions, from men and women alike, about the proper texture of a good loaf. Most men seem to prefer a close-textured, heavier bread while the women favored a lighter bread with more air holes. Here is a recipe given to me by Mrs. Hazel Cook of Golden Ridge Farm, from Portugal Cove, for a close-textured molasses brown bread. This same bread was sent from Newfoundland, sliced and buttered, every week, to a friend of mine, when she was at school in Boston. It was supposed to have keeping qualities, but not for Penny. It always disappeared, even though she hid it in a different place, whenever she left her room.

Mrs. Hazel Cook's Molasses Brown Bread

5 cups white flour
2 lbs. whole wheat flour, approx. 4 cups [907g]
1 cup molasses
½ cup white sugar
2 eggs [optional]
2 tsp. salt
¼ cup butter [soft]
warm water, enough to mix batter to a stiff dough
2 envelopes dry yeast

Put ¼ cup sugar in 1 cup warm water. Add yeast. Mix dry ingredients together with butter. Make a well in the mixture and add yeast which has stood at least ten minutes. Add molasses and eggs. Add warm water to make a stiff dough, kneading 10 minutes until it is smooth and pliable. Let rise in a warm place for at least two hours. (Cover bowl of dough with a clean cloth.) Punch it down again and let rise for 10 or 15 minutes. Put in pans and let rise for 1 hour. Bake at 350° F (175° C) for 1 hour. Yields 4 medium loaves.

The classic Newfoundland dish, fish and brewis, is composed of salt cod, hardtack biscuits and salt pork. Fish and brewis reflects perfectly the culinary facts of life in Newfoundland. Until the second half of this century, everything was imported from Canada or overseas on slow-moving boats. Thus, pork had to be salted and biscuits had to be dry and hard for keeping. (The most common imported fruits, by the way, were dates and raisins.) The biscuits and cod are soaked overnight. Then the cod is boiled, and flaked with a fork; the hardtack biscuits are drained, heated and added to the cod, and the fried scrunchions (crispy bits of pork fat) are poured over the dish. There are variations to this theme, but essentially this is it. It is still a most popular dish, along with seal-flipper pie and Jiggs dinner.

Newfoundland Jiggs Dinner

Very traditional; most groceries in Newfoundland have a barrel of salt beef somewhere on the premises. The Town and Country Restaurant in St. John's serves a Jiggs Dinner at least once a week.

Soak pork and beef in cold water overnight. In the morning, drain and add fresh water. Bring to a boil and simmer for 2 hours. Prepare vegetables for cooking. Quarter potatoes, cut turnip and carrots rather coarsely, cut cabbage in wedges. Add potatoes, cabbage and turnip, cook just until they are done.

Jiggs dinner is usually eaten with pease pudding.

Serves 6

2 lbs. of corned beef or salt beef ribs [907g]
½ lb. salt pork [227g]
8 potatoes
6 carrots
1 medium turnip
1 medium cabbage

17

Pease Pudding

1 cup yellow split peas
salt and pepper to taste
butter

Wash peas. Drain, and put them in a pudding bag made of flour sack material. A jelly bag will do. Tie bag rather loosely so peas will have room to expand. Boil peas in the same water as your Jiggs dinner, for the same amount of time, approximately 3 hours. When cooked, remove peas from bag and mash with butter and salt and pepper. Serve along with other vegetables in the Jiggs dinner.

Great-Grandmother's Gingerbread Recipe

I found this handwritten in a Columbus Ladies Association cookbook published in Newfoundland in 1920.

Set oven at 350 ° F [175° C].

½ cup sugar
½ cup butter and lard mixed
1 egg
1 cup molasses
2½ cups sifted flour
1½ tsp. soda
1 tbsp. cinnamon
1 tbsp. ginger [another tbsp. won't hurt]
1 tsp. cloves
½ tsp. salt
1 cup hot water

Cream shortening and sugar, add beaten egg and molasses. Mix well. Sift dry ingredients together. Add flour with spices and soda carefully to butter mixture, mixing well. Add hot water last, mixing well. Bake in a greased shallow pan for 45 minutes.

18

Foxberry (or Cranberry) & Deep Apple Pie

Cut butter and shortening into flour. Sprinkle with water and mix lightly. Roll out dough. Makes 1 crust.

Dough

1½ cups flour
 ½ cup shortening
 ¼ cup salted butter
 ¼ cup ice water

Mix filling ingredients together and put into buttered baking dish. Place rolled out dough on top. Sprinkle crust with cinnamon and sugar. Bake about 30 to 40 minutes at 375° F (190° C). The fruit will cook much quicker than the crust.

Filling

  6 apples peeled, cored and sliced
1 - 2 cups of cranberries, depending on how much you have at hand
½- ¾ cup brown sugar, maple sugar or honey.
       [The more cranberries you have, the more sugar you need.]

2. Something More than Oatmeal and Herring

The Scottish Hebrides were never, at any time, the center of the civilized world. They were the home of ancient and valiant Highland clans, Macleans, Macneils and MacKenzies, renowned for their independence, pride and fighting spirit. But not one of the lairds of these clans, on their rocky remote islands, could ever be compared to a pope in Rome, a king in France, or even a prime minister in London. Yet the chief of the Clan Macneil, who lived in Castlebay, a small hamlet within the Island of Barra which is part of the Hebrides, felt no sense of inferiority. Every night, a herald would mount the battlements of the laird's castle, sound his trumpet, and proclaim: "Hear oh ye peoples! Listen oh ye nations! The Great Macneil of Barra has finished his dinner. The other princes of the earth may now dine."

Hector MacSheumais Macneil of Barra, a descendant of that proud laird, was one of the first Highlanders to come to Nova Scotia; he and his family settled in Cape Breton in 1802. The Macneils of Cape Breton did not end their dinner with the blast of the trumpet, but the food they ate was indubitably the same as their aristocratic fore-father's in Kisimul Castle — oatmeal and herring. This was the nutritious but austere diet of the Highland Celt and Lowland Angle since the beginning of Scotland. When Samuel Johnson toured the Highlands in the eighteenth century, the lairds' pipers in the castles he visited ceremoniously led him through the baronial halls to dine on the same.

Oatmeal and herring stood the Nova Scotia settlers in good stead. Certainly it was a factor in their survival on the immigrant ships or floating coffins that brought them to this country in the early nineteenth century. The voyage could last as long as six weeks; the water was foul; dysentery, cholera, and typhus were endemic. But a list of the survivors on the St. Lawrence that docked in Ships Harbour, Cape Breton, included four Highlanders in their late eighties; a census of the newly arrived Highlanders in the Pictou district noted six people over seventy. Centuries of vitamin D intake and healthful helpings of oatmeal roughage (the oatmeal then was not like the refined pap we eat today) enabled their tough bodies to resist the worst. They saw no reason to discontinue their diet when they arrived in Canada, so they seeded their oats; and of course, herring was even more abundant in Canada than in the old country.

The Scotch (as they are called in Canada) did not escape from the horrors of settling new land. Blight, destructive frost, the task of clearing the spruce off their fields led to misery and starvation. The only way for them to survive was to continue as their ancestors had done, and make virtue out of necessity by living a frugal life. But no matter how austere an existence they led, it never overcame their other virtue, hospitality.

Once upon a time, in the early days of the Highland settlement on Cape Breton Island, a young man found himself too tired and hungry to continue his walk from Cow Bay to Lower Washabuck. He stopped at a small farmhouse and asked for shelter. The farmhouse belonged to a poor widow with five young children; her poverty appalled the young man so much, that he tried to refuse her offer of an evening meal. But she was adamant and miserably embarrassed by his denial of her hospitality. There was nothing else for him to do but sit at her table. She went out to the backyard for several minutes, and he heard the most terrible shrieking coming from the barnyard. Twenty minutes later, she presented him with a plate of two boiled pig's ears and one tail. While he ate them, without much enjoyment, the agonized cries continued. The lady had cut the expendable parts off her living pig, in order not to break the Cape Breton code of hospitality.

Less pathetic is this story told to me by a Tait from Toronto, with some Highland blood, about his father, Canadian born, who had an uncle, a Presbyterian minister living in Scotland. The uncle begged his nephew to visit his manse, church and parish — all were on what the nephew described later as a "middle sized rock" in Sutherland County. When he finally got there, the nephew was somewhat daunted by his uncle's hospitality. Porridge for breakfast, porridge for lunch, and porridge and a little herring at 5:30. And then everyone went to bed. The Canadian Tait had risen in the world, gastronomically speaking; he even had a mother (with French blood) who secretly poured sherry in the trifle. Understandably he left earlier than he had planned. At his departure his uncle thrust his hand into a tin of tea leaves, pulled out a five pound note and tucked it in his nephew's pocket. If the minister had plucked an emerald from the right eye of a sacred idol at Benares, and sent it to him second-class mail, the nephew could not have been more astounded. His aunt must have been surprised as well, when she found out. Several days later, when he was in Oxford, the nephew received a note from his uncle asking for the return of the five pounds. Hospitality is part of the Scot's code, never prodigality.

There was no herring, no porridge, or pig's ears on Mrs. Earle Boyd's table, in her house at Brook Street, Halifax, when I ate lunch there. Jean Boyd has Highland and Lowland Scotch ancestors; her family, the Wrights, believe they are descendants of the first James Wright who settled in Bedford Basin in 1826 and had Wright's Cove named after him. Jean's hospitality was equal in spirit to that poor widow from Cape Breton, but she lacked the shrieking pig in the barn. We started off our lunch with a Tio Pepe sherry. Life in Nova Scotia has changed for the better over 200 years. Scotch delicacies have not disappeared from the Boyds' diet, however. Earle Boyd, who is principal of J.L. Ilsley High School in Halifax, manages to eat three or four of Jean's Cape Breton oatcakes, (sometimes called "asbestos shingles" by Lunenburgers), for breakfast. Our lunch was a rich chowder, with chopped shrimp, haddock and lobster, Jean's oatcakes, homemade brown bread, scones with butter, and a German Niersteiner wine.

We were silent as we ate the dessert, apple dumplings and whipped cream, although we had chatted like magpies until their arrival. Perfection on the plate needed our reverence, and silent attention was one way of giving homage. It was often the custom, in the more severe of the old Scotch households, not to talk during meal time. Some say that because of a dour attitude to life, conversation was forbidden during any sensual activity. If however, they were eating apple dumplings and cream, their reason for silence is perfectly understandable.

Jean's hospitality reaches its epitome at Christmas. Every morsel at the Boyd's annual Christmas party has been prepared, sometimes weeks before, by Jean, who loves cooking. Her critical faculty is acute. We were discussing what a certain Haligonian put in her trifle, and I asked if the custard was usually homemade. Jean shrugged, "I don't like to say, but my own custard is better."

The Boyds' Christmas spread includes Jean's fruitcakes, which she bakes over pans of hot water in her oven, shortbread, of course, and cherry surprises, homemade mincemeat tarts, decorated sugar cookies, her famous trifle, and petit fours. But those are only the sweet things. There's always a baked ham, shrimp curry salad, sweet and sour meatballs, aspics, and scalloped potatoes. (Not to mention the oatcakes and some cheese, and her homemade bread and scones.)

Jean Boyd's Scotch Oatcakes

They are marvelous with butter, cheese or just plain with a cup of tea.

Mix dry ingredients and cut in shortening. Add water and form into a ball of dough. Roll out. Cut into 2 inch (5 cm) squares. Bake at about 375° F (190° C) until golden brown.

3 cups rolled oats
3 cups flour
1 cup sugar
2 tsp. salt
2 cups shortening
¼ to ⅓ cup water, enough to hold dough together

23

Rich Fish Chowder

The Scotch in Nova Scotia have come a long way from oatmeal and herring. I never tasted a better chowder.

¼ lb. salt pork, cut very fine [113 g]
2 medium onions [diced]
1 cup water
3 medium potatoes [diced]
1 cup diced shrimp
1 cup scallops, cut in quarters with scissors
1 cup lobster meat
1 cup haddock fillet, cut up
2 cups light cream
1 15 oz can evaporated milk [426 ml]
salt and pepper to taste

Render salt pork, and drain off most of the fat. Add onions and sauté until transparent. Add water and then potatoes to the salt pork and onion mixture. Simmer until potato absorbs water and is cooked. Add seafood, milk, and cream. Simmer just until fish is done. But do not bring the chowder to a boil. Salt and pepper to taste.

Jean Boyd's Perfect Trifle

Some think trifle is strictly an English dessert, but the Scots have claimed it as theirs for centuries.

one sponge cake or white cake [preferably homemade]
½ cup of dry sherry
1 recipe light custard
1 box frozen raspberries or strawberries [defrosted]
½ cup of whipping cream, sweetened

Place cake, cut in cubes, in a large bowl. Sprinkle ¼ cup of the sherry over cake. Pour custard over cake. Pour defrosted fruit and juice over custard. Sprinkle rest of sherry over the fruit. Cover the fruit with the sweetened whipped cream. Let this set for at least 12 hours. This may be made in the morning, for an evening party.

Light Custard

Beat egg yolks, add sugar and cornstarch to yolks a little at a time. Scald milk. Pour hot (not boiling) milk slowly into egg yolk and sugar mixture and cook in double boiler until it begins to thicken. The sauce should not be too thick. Add vanilla. Cool.

3 egg yolks
¼ cup sugar
1 tbsp. cornstarch
2⅓ cups milk
1 tsp. vanilla flavoring

Trifle Cake

One of the qualities of good trifle is the way the cake soaks up the sherry. This plain white cake has a rather coarse texture that is ideal for drinking up liquor. I don't like it for anything else except trifle. But I don't like trifle without this particular cake. I use about three quarters of this cake for Jean Boyd's trifle and freeze the rest.

Cream butter and sugar together. Add eggs mixing well. Now add flour and milk alternately, in three installments with the flour last. Add baking powder and vanilla, mixing well. Pour in a round or square pan. Bake at 350° F (175° C) for 30 to 40 minutes.

¼ lb butter [113 g]
1 cup fruit sugar
2 eggs
2 cups flour
¾ cup milk
3 tsp. baking powder
1 tsp. vanilla

A Whole-Wheat Bread with Oatmeal in it

This is rather a sweet tasting bread. You don't need to eat it with jam. Makes three large round loaves or four smaller round loaves.

2 envelopes of dry yeast
2 cups lukewarm water
1 tbsp. sugar
1 cup flour
½ cup processed [not instant] rolled oats

Sprinkle yeast in water (use large bowl). Add tablespoon of sugar. Let mixture sit for 10 minutes, until yeast is activated. Add 1 cup of flour to yeast mixture and let stand for half an hour.

In the meantime, cook ½ cup of processed rolled oats, in 1 cup of boiling water about 5 minutes.

1½ cups lukewarm water
1 tsp. salt
1 cup brown sugar
cooked rolled oats
½ cup shortening
½ cup molasses
3 cups white flour
6 cups whole wheat flour
[more white flour can be added if the dough is really too sticky to handle]

Add to the bowl containing yeast and flour.

Knead about 10 minutes, until dough loses its stickiness. Put into a large greased bowl, cover bowl with a towel, and let the dough rise for about 2 hours in an unheated oven, or until its bulk has doubled. Form into oblong or round free-standing loaves. Let the loaves rise for about one more hour. Bake at 350° F (175° C) for one hour. Brush crust with butter when baked.

Maritime Codfish Cakes

very light and tender

[from an old stained recipe book]

Flake 1½ lb. of cooked codfish (680 g). Add an equal amount of mashed potatoes (3 medium potatoes) that have been whipped with an electric beater. Add ¼ tsp. ginger. Mix with 2 tablespoons of cream and two egg yolks. Shape into round flat cakes and dust them with a little flour. Cook them in butter and oil until they are brown and crisp on both sides. (A tablespoon of chopped parsley mixed in the fish and potato mixture will do it no harm.) Eat with lemon wedges. Smoked cod is also good, done in this manner.

Easy Seville Marmalade

Boil oranges and lemon in water until very soft, about ½ hour. Remove from water. Cut in little pieces, letting water simmer all the while. Add sugar to the water. Let cook for 5 minutes. Throw in oranges and lemon, pits and all, and let cook for 20 minutes or until 220° F (105° C). Pour into sterilized jars.

You may cook it longer so that the color will turn amber, but you will have less marmalade.

This recipe works better if you do 6 oranges at a time.

12 bitter oranges [Seville type — they appear in the stores in February]
16 or 17 cups water
9 to 10 cups sugar
1 lemon

Backwoods Pie

Pastry

1½ cups whole-wheat flour
¼ cup butter
½ cup shortening
1 tbsp. sugar and a little ice water

Make a pie-crust shell. Place in 400° F (205° C) oven for 10 minutes. Make sure you prick it with a fork and cover bottom with foilwrap so it won't puff up in the oven. Let the crust cool.

Filling

1 cup brown sugar
1½ cups maple syrup
5 oz. milk [142 ml]
4 egg yolks
2 tbsp. butter
4 beaten egg whites

After the first 5 ingredients are well mixed, fold in 4 beaten egg whites. Sprinkle or grate a little nutmeg over pie-crust shell. Pour liquid into shell and bake at 350° F (175° C) for 25 to 30 minutes. Sweet, gooey and crunchy.

Mrs. Bell's Scones

2 cups flour
2 tsp. baking powder
¾ tsp. salt
3 tbsp. sugar
⅓ tsp. soda
5 full tbsp. butter
⅓ cup currants,
   washed and dried
⅔ cup thick sour cream
1 egg separated
   cinnamon

Sift flour before measuring, then sift together dry ingredients. Rub in butter and currants. Mix yolk with cream; add to make a soft dough. Mix well and knead lightly 2 or 3 times on lightly floured pastry board or cloth. Pat out ½" thick (1.25 cm). Cut in circles about 4" or 5" in diameter (12.5 cm). Mark out into quarters with back of silver knife. Brush lightly with unbeaten egg white. Sprinkle a little sugar with cinnamon on top. Bake in 425° F (220° C) oven 15 to 18 minutes (or less) until well raised and golden brown.

Steak and Kidney Pie

Cut the beef in 1½″ (3.8 cm) cubes and dredge them in the flour. Fry salt pork bits in the bottom of a heavy casserole until they are crisp. Add more fat, butter or oil if necessary and then brown meat and onions. Remove any particularly fatty pork bits.

Now heat brandy in a separate container with a handle. Light the warmed brandy and pour it over the meat, letting it burn as much as possible. Pour stock and water over meat and add salt, pepper, mustard. Let the mixture cook for 2 to 3 hours, adding carrots and parsnips about 20 minutes before you take the pot off the stove.

In the meantime, remove the filament from the kidneys and very slightly brown them in a chunk of butter. The kidneys should be quite raw in the middle when you remove them to the **cooled** steak and broth mixture. If the mixture seems thin, thicken with a **beurre manié** (flour and a little butter rolled into a ball) or a paste made with flour and water. Taste for seasoning; add more salt, pepper and mustard if you think it necessary. Lightly brown the whole mushrooms and add them to the mixture.

Transfer meat and liquid to an earthenware or glass casserole and top with rolled out pastry. Cut a hole in the centre of the pastry and insert a funnel of foilwrap, so the juices won't spill over.

The final baking may be done a day later. Bake in a 350° F (175° C) oven for about 45 minutes. (You might have to use the broiler to brown the crust at the end.)

rich pastry dough, enough for one 9″ crust [23 cm] [prepare first and put it aside in a cool place]

2 lbs. round steak or blade steak [907 g]
½ lb. salt pork, cut in small cubes [227 g]
flour as needed
2 large onions chopped
⅓ cup brandy
2 cups brown stock
2 cups water
salt and pepper
2 tbsp. French mustard
2 carrots
3 parsnips
1½ lbs. veal or lamb kidneys [680 g]
½ lb. mushrooms [leave caps whole] [227 g]

29

3. Mrs. Zinck and Green Shutters

A few years ago I came across a coil-back green and white cook book. The cover had a cartoon of a fat man with a napkin around his ears, stuffing himself with fried chicken and pies; underneath was written, "If you want to lose weight don't open this book." The title was, "Green Shutters Cook Book." On the inside page there was another drawing — of a big clapboard house, with a wide old-fashioned verandah, and shutters framing the upstairs windows. The house was Green Shutters, on Mahone Bay, Lunenburg County, Nova Scotia, and the recipes were from the kitchen of Mrs. Hilda Zinck.

I was intrigued. Many of Mrs. Zinck's recipes were Lunenburg County's German style, wilted lettuce salad, hodge podge, sauerkraut, spare ribs and rye bread, but her scones and shortbread showed how Nova Scotia's Anglo Celt heritage influenced Lunenburg German cooking for the past two hundred years. I also fell in love with the drawing of Green Shutters — it was every writer's childhood dream house, from L.M. Montgomery to my own. Three years after the discovery of Mrs. Zinck's book, I had the chance to go down to Halifax where she lived , and talk to her about cooking, and Green Shutters.

Mrs. Zinck, a grey-haired lady with a gentle manner, worried very much about the comfort of others. Her happiest years were at Green Shutters. When she told me how she loved working side by side with her husband, Lem, her voice trembled and her eyes misted. Yet the life she described is hardly the kind most people would regret; up at six to prepare breakfast for her guests, and still in the kitchen past midnight, rolling pastry for the next day's pies. Mrs. Zinck and her husband were owners of the Green Shutters Tourist Home — so well-known during the Fifties that Sunday traffic on the road to Green Shutters would be blocked for miles; locals and tourists all wanted to sample Mrs. Zinck's cooking. Her kitchen was photographed by newspapers; national magazines wrote about her meals; and Mrs. Zinck appeared on television.

She told me what it was like to be a guest at Green Shutters. "Once a man and his family came in past the dinner hour, really cranky, don't you know, because he had been driving a long time, and they were so hungry." Mrs. Zinck had a Lunenburg lilt and phrasing in her speech. "I brought them a tray of my special rhubarb juice, and asked Mary, the wonderful girl who helped me, to run out and pick some vegetables in the garden. Although it was too late to offer the guests the set meal, I had a good supply of lamb chops and fresh fish. By the time they had eaten relishes, barley bread, coleslaw, blueberry muffins and Green Shutter soup (everything homemade) the fish and chops were all ready. When the man tasted the baby peas and carrots Mary had picked, he asked how come they were the best he ever tasted. Why, I said, they were still growing when you rang my door bell ."

Mrs. Zinck was born near the Lahave River in Lunenburg County. Her family, the Grimms, (directly related to the famous brothers), are descendants of the early settlers who came from Germany, over two hundred years ago, and named Lunenburg after the German seaport. Mrs. Zinck's musical accent, her love of good food, and strong feeling for beauty and order are typical of Lunenburg people. Not only did she do all the cooking at Green Shutters, but she tended flower beds which were the admiration of the neighborhood. Her husband wallpapered all the rooms in Green Shutters himself and took pride in keeping the house as handsome as when it was first built — over one hundred years before. Captain Roland Harris, who wrote the historical notes in the Green Shutters Cook Book, comments, "In Lunenburg County, fresh paint, neat gardens, and well-kept fields are worn ... as a national dress. Unpainted buildings, unkept grounds, may well invite the critical glance, the whispered comment."

Interest in and love of good food, as well as pride in well-kept homes, have been part of Lunenburg's tradition since the first settlers came from Frisia and the German Palatinate in 1750. The German flavor is still detectable.   Although the Lunenburgers borrowed the Newfoundland habit of eating salt fish with pork scraps, (scrunchions in Newfoundland), they added a very Teutonic cup of sour cream to the mixture, and made it Deutsch, or German, style. Their Scotch neighbors, wondering at what they were doing, unkindly named it Dutch Mess. And the recipe is called Dutch Mess to this day. Turnip Kraut and Sauerkraut (Mrs. Zinck's family put them up at the rise and fall of the moon), hot coleslaws, caraway seeds sprinkled on and about vegetables and cakes, and rye and barley bread are typical of Lunenburg German cooking.

However, Mrs. Zinck's cookbook is a perfect example of the culinary cross-pollination that occurs in our country. Besides the Dutch Mess and sauerkraut soup, Mrs. Zinck gives recipes for cottage pudding, scones and tea cakes, all Anglo-Celtic dishes which form the major part of Nova Scotia cooking tradition. The Germans and the Scotch lived side by side for two hundred years — naturally their cooking styles mingled. Sometimes the Scotch culinary style goes beyond what Lunenburgers consider fit to eat. A Lunenburg storekeeper took some Scottish oatcakes home for his wife to try. She served them to the Lutheran pastor who remarked, "When I want asbestos shingles, I'll buy them at the hardware store."

The German Lunenburgers were fishermen and farmers who worked hard and needed daily about five thousand calories more than we do to survive. Mrs. Zinck's mother made eight loaves of barley and white bread each day for her family of eleven children. Hilda was the eldest of eight girls and like most eldest daughters in those days, naturally took over much of the cooking chores from her mother. Chores is not the right word. Both she and her mother loved cooking, and Hilda was allowed to make her own mistakes. She said "Why the first batch of brownies I made was tough enough to knock a grown man down. But my mother never complained."

After her marriage it was not a great jump from feeding her family on the farm to cooking for the guests at Green Shutters. At least Mrs. Zinck felt that way. When she wasn't preparing breakfast, lunch and dinner or weeding her garden, she passed the time packing two-layer brownies, Jumbles and June Bugs in individual picnic boxes, for guests taking afternoon tea at Green Shutters. I asked Mrs. Zinck if she made the bread as well. "Well I guess so," said she, indignantly, "even the croutons floating on the soup were homemade."

Mrs. Zinck was the manager of the Saraguay, a private club on the shores of the North West Arm, near Halifax. The Saraguay, with its impersonal dining room and vaguely "contemporary" architecture might be a country club or community hall anywhere: Edmonton, Toronto or Poughkeepsie, N.Y. No building could be more of a contrast to the rambling, welcoming Green Shutters, so distinctly Nova Scotia in style. Mrs. Zinck lived in an apartment on the grounds of the Saraguay. She had no kitchen of her own. Her managing duties allowed her no time for cooking in the Saraguay's kitchen — it was all she could do to see that the chef used fresh apples instead of canned, for the pies. She asked me to be her guest at dinner and ordered a special salad dressing and hot coleslaw Lunenburg style.

Green Shutters does not exist anymore. When Mrs. Zinck and her husband were at their happiest, (they were even planning to add cabins in the same style as the main house, for the overflow guests), Mr. Zinck died of a heart attack. Mrs. Zinck carried on with her Lunenburg cooking at Green Shutters for six more years, but there was too much work for one person. In the winter she could get no one to shovel her driveway. In the summer Mrs. Zinck, alone, was unable to cope with the crowds. Hiring extra help was no solution. No one wanted to keep up Mrs. Zinck's standards, because it meant a fifteen hour day, seven day week, during the season. Only somebody like her husband could give Green Shutters the care and devotion it needed; running a guest house and restaurant is traditionally a family business, and Mrs. Zinck had no children — strangers aren't the same. She sold Green Shutters to a local merchant who bulldozed the one hundred years old house and built two houses of indeterminate style in its place. Nothing remains except the drawing of Green Shutters on the cookbook, some newspaper clippings and Mrs. Zinck's memories.

"Someday," she said, "I'm going to buy a little house, plant some vegetables and flowers, and rent out a room or two. It won't be like

Green Shutters, my health is not what it should be, but at least I'll have my own kitchen."

Even though Green Shutters no longer exists, Mrs. Zinck's Lunenburg style of cooking lives on. You can still eat Solomon Gundy (a marinated herring), Dutch Mess, potato pies and krishelo, (patties made from curds, cream and caraway seeds) in Lunenburg homes, if not the restaurants. People still put down their own sauerkraut, and bake their pies and cakes. Mrs. Zinck gave me a jar of her sister's homemade chili sauce, and bottled green beans from their vegetable garden, so I would have some edible proof.

Hodge-Podge

A particularly delicious way of cooking young vegetables. This has been a German Lunenburg specialty for the past 200 years. You don't need any meat dish to accompany hodge podge; the salt pork makes hodge podge filling enough for a main course.

carrots
onion
new green beans and peas
salt pork
small new potatoes
butter and cream [sweet or sour]
  minimum amount 1 cup
salt and pepper

There are no quantities given. Just keep adding vegetables according to the number of people eating. If you have cauliflower and chives growing in your garden, add the first to the boiling water, and sprinkle on the latter, just before serving.

Cover carrots and onion with boiling water. Add salt, allowing 1 tsp. to 1 quart (1.14 l) of water. Add other vegetables, giving each one just enough time to cook. Use as little water as possible. Add new peas last.

Dice salt pork, and fry to a golden brown, while vegetables are cooking. When vegetables are done, add at least one cup of cream, and lots of butter. Toss in crisped bits of salt pork.

I love this recipe because it would be pure Newfoundland if it didn't have that cup of cream. The cream makes it Lunenburg German.

Rhubarb Juice

Much cheaper than fresh orange juice and just as healthy, as well as being delicious. Mrs. Zinck says this was a great favorite with her guests.

Keep in refrigerator. This is ready for use when cold.

2½ lbs. rhubarb [1.13 kg]
80 oz. water [2.27 l]
Cut rhubarb and stew in water; strain through cheesecloth [I just use an ordinary strainer and potato masher]. Add:
1¼ cups sugar
juice of 2 lemons
juice of 1 orange
4 whole cloves.

Cucumber Salad

Sour cream is a basic in German cooking. This simple cucumber salad may be found in many Lunenburg homes at supper time.

Peel and slice about 6 medium-sized cucumbers. Put into dish and sprinkle each layer with a little salt. Press with a heavy weight for 2 hours or longer. Drain well. Cut up some new onion quite fine and add to cucumbers. Mix with the dressing. These proportions are approximate; sugar and vinegar are added to taste.

Dressing

1 cup sour cream [slightly whipped]
½ cup [more or less] sugar
⅓ cup vinegar
little pepper

35

Sugar Plum Fruit Cake

This is one of the best fruit cakes I've ever tasted. The apricots make it unusual. I don't like pineapple, so I just added an extra cup of apricots instead. I also added an extra half cup of brandy.

1½ cups dried apricots
¼ cup honey
1 cup seeded raisins
2 cups seedless raisins
½ cup brandy or grape juice
1 cup diced candied pineapple
1 cup candied cherries, halved
1½ cups diced citron
1 cup diced candied orange peel
1 cup sliced dates
1 cup slivered blanched almonds
1 cup coarsely chopped walnuts
1 cup coarsely chopped pecans
1 cup butter or shortening
1¼ cups brown sugar
4 eggs
2 cups flour
1 tsp. salt
½ tsp. mace
¼ tsp. cloves
¼ tsp. soda
1 tsp. cinnamon

Rinse apricots; cover with water and boil 10 minutes. Drain, cool and chop. Combine with honey in small pan and bring to boiling point. Cover and let stand until cool. Rinse both seeded and seedless raisins and drain well. Chop seeded raisins. Turn apricots and honey into large bowl. Add raisins and pour brandy over all ingredients. Cover and let stand overnight. Candied fruit, citron, dates and nuts may be prepared and added to this bowl the same day, but do not mix so that candied fruits soak in brandy and honey.

The next day, cream shortening and sugar thoroughly. Beat in eggs, one at a time. Sift flour, salt, soda and spices and mix thoroughly into creamed mixture. Now mix fruits in large bowl by lifting from bottom of bowl with large spoon. Pour batter over fruits and mix very well. Turn into greased pans lined with greased brown or wax paper. Use one 10-inch (25.4 cm) tube cake pan or a large loaf pan. Bake in a slow oven 275° F (135° C) for 4-5 hours. Makes 6½ - 7 lbs. cake (3.2 kg). After cake has cooled completely wrap in cloth dipped in brandy, and then wrap in aluminum foil. Store cake in tin to age for four or more weeks.

Bacon and Egg Mousse

Cut ¼ lb. (113g) of side bacon in small pieces and fry until crisp. Drain and cool.

Boil 4 eggs till they are hard.

Combine in a heatproof bowl 2 tbsp. gelatine and ½ cup of water; let stand for 5 minutes. Place in a pan of hot water and heat until gelatin is dissolved. Keep warm until needed.

Measure into a large bowl 1 cup of mayonnaise; gradually stir in 1 cup undiluted evaporated milk or light cream, ¼ cup lemon juice. Quickly stir in hot gelatin; stir in cooked bacon, ½ tsp. salt, pepper, 4 coarsely chopped hard-cooked eggs, ¾ cup finely chopped celery, ¼ cup finely chopped green pepper, ½ cup green peas.

Fold mixture well and chill, stirring occasionally so that solids stay distributed throughout. When just beginning to jell turn into a lightly oiled mold. Chill until set. Garnish with pimento.

Green Shutters Calla Lilies

Beat until thick and light 1 egg and a few grains of salt. Beat in gradually ¼ cup of sugar and 1 tsp. of vanilla or any other flavoring. Fold in alternately 6 tbsp. of flour and 1½ tsp. of cold water. Drop batter in small mounds on greased baking sheet, having no more than 5 or 6 mounds on each sheet; with a spoon spread each mound into a round, about 4″ (10 cm) in diameter. Bake in a pre-heated oven, 375° F (190° C) just to a light golden color – about 5 minutes. Working at the open oven, or while they are still warm, loosen one at a time, turn upside down and shape into a cone. Place on a cake cooler and when cold and ready to serve fill with whipped cream sweetened and flavored. Dot with jelly to resemble a calla bloom.

To vary the filling add some powdered instant coffee.

Dutch Mess Green Shutter Style

1 lb. of salt cod [454 g]
6 large potatoes
2 or more large onions
1 cup of diced salt pork
1 cup of sweet or sour cream
   pepper to taste

Break up codfish in strips and soak overnight in cold water. If too salty, change water and let it soak a little longer. Peel potatoes and cut into bite size pieces. Put potatoes and fish in pot and cook until potatoes are done. Drain well. Fry pork and onions until a golden brown. Add cream and combine. Pour this over the fish and potatoes. Serve hot with applesauce, fried apples or any favorite relish. (Any leftover from this dish may be mashed, and with the addition of a beaten egg and some finely chopped parsley, made into fish cakes.)

Smoked cod may be used instead of salt. In that case, soaking the cod is not necessary.

Lunenburg Hot Lobster Salad

Sauté onion in a little butter. Mix flour, mustard and vinegar. Add cream and sugar, stirring, and pour over lobster meat. Let simmer to thicken. Serve in pastry shells, or in crisp lettuce cups.

3 cups lobster, cut up
1 onion
1 tsp. dry mustard
2 tbsp. vinegar
1 tbsp. flour
¾ cup sweet cream
1 small tsp. sugar
   salt and pepper to taste

4. Poutine à Trou et Chiard

The land facing the Northumberland Straits in New Brunswick is flat, and when the day is unusually clear you can see a blue mist far out on the water, which in reality is the western edge of Prince Edward Island. Looking at the sea from Mme. Alozia Léger's house on the land side of the highway, you'd think both land and sea are on the same level. But the shore is a good drop below, with few sandy beaches to attract tourists. This is fisherman's country rather than vacation land, and Mme. Léger's husband, a fisherman, is more concerned with the lobster catch than the amount of jellyfish in the sea; the latter upset the odd swimmer in July. The Légers are New Brunswick Acadian and sound the 'r' in their name, unlike the Governor-General who is from Quebec. Not only do Acadians speak French with a different intonation; some of their culinary specialties are virtually unknown to a Quebecois. One of these is pâté rapé or chiard, as the Légers call it, which is kind of a potato pudding, made with salt pork, grated potato, and then baked in a shallow pan in the oven for a couple of hours. Acadian fishermen, farmers and lumberjacks have eaten it, hot or cold, for centuries, with molasses, marinades (chili sauces) or more recently, ketchup. Mme. Léger offered me some when I visited her — she and her husband are slim, hardworking people who need all the calories they can get. More sedentary people like myself should refrain from second helpings.

A version of pâté rapé is poutine rapée, made with basically the same ingredients but formed into large balls and cooked in water, like dumplings. Poutines are so popular in the Moncton area that the sign POUTINE RAPEE A APPORTER or TAKE-OUT POUTINE RAPEE is frequently seen at drive-in stands. Mme. Léger's daughter, Berenice, who is a teacher, calls them dirty snowballs.

The Légers' freshly painted white clapboard house is one hundred and fifty years old. Mme. Léger has her flowerbed in front (asparagus fern and yellow dahlias) and her vegetable garden in the back. She grows

40

corn, cabbage, green beans, onions, and carrots, among other things. The vegetables are for the Légers' winter soup. Mme. Léger scrapes, washes and trims a combination of the vegetables in August, and puts the quantity needed for a pot of soup in a multitude of separate plastic bags, which she freezes. In December when she makes soup, she takes one plastic bag out of the freezer and throws the prepared vegetables into a boiling pot of water, containing potatoes, summer savory and a meat bone. There is something satisfying about eating winter soup with summer vegetables.

The Légers' front door opens directly into the most important room of the house, a kitchen, dining and family area furnished with an old-fashioned stove, dining table and rocking chairs decorated with cushions embroidered by Mme. Léger, who is also an expert quilt-maker. This house design is typical of many of the older dwellings in Quebec and New Brunswick. The parlor or living room is smaller and leads off from the central room. Mme. Leger's pride and joy, her flowering hoya plant, sits in front of its south window.

The pièce de résistance of Acadian cooking is poutine à trou. Some people might call it an apple dumpling, but it's different from any I've eaten. The concept behind poutine à trou is ingenious. If you see one baked, it looks like a perfect cylinder of gilded pastry with a little hole on top. Straightforward enough, but there is a mystery inside, and you have to sink your teeth into it to find the secret.

Poutine à Trou

Here is how Mme. Léger goes about making poutine à trou. She sits down at her kitchen table and peels an apple with a small paring knife, never a peeler. Mme. Léger hates waste and peels very thinly; the red apple skin goes round and round, never breaking off till her knife has stripped the fruit clean. After chopping the apple up in little pieces, she places a portion of it, as well as some muscat raisins, on a round

piece of pastry dough that she has previously rolled out. Pinching and pleating, she works the dough over the fruit, so that a completely closed ball is created. Then she takes an important step. Mme. Léger turns the ball over and pushes a hole in the bottom, her finger making a slight corkscrew motion through the dough. The trou is formed. The dumpling is placed on a baking pan with its chimney hole facing the ceiling. One teaspoon of sugar syrup is sent down the chimney and only when the dumpling is baked and cooled is the rest of the sauce poured inside. Poutine à trou must be completely dry on the outside, so that its juiciness will come as a complete surprise. M. Léger takes poutine à trou with him on the fishing boat and doesn't want to handle a sticky, gluey dumpling. It's de rigueur to eat poutine à trou with your hands.

Dough

    4 cups flour [all purpose]
    4 tsp. baking powder
    1 tsp. salt
    1 cup shortening or butter
1¼ cup milk

For 18 dumplings, the smallest quantity of poutine à trou that Mme. Léger makes at any given time. (She has a 100 pound (45 kg) flour bin in the kitchen and makes bread and rolls three times a week.) Mix as for pastry and roll out.

Sauce

1¼ cup white sugar
1¼ cup water
    lump of butter or margarine
    size of an egg yolk

Combine ingredients and bring to a boil on low heat.

Filling

    4 or 5 cooking apples [peeled, cored and chopped as described]
12 oz. [340 g] bag of seeded muscat raisins

Bake at 350° F (175° C) for about 40 minutes.

Chicken Fricot

Find two hens and chop each one in four (after they are killed). Cover them with cold water and ten chopped onions — salt to taste. Boil three hours, or until the meat comes off the bones. Put in the refrigerator until fat comes to top. Skim off all the fat.

Remove as much skin as possible from the chicken, and take out the big bones from the soup. Now put ¼ cup of dried summer savory in the soup. Simmer one hour. Chop 5 potatoes and 3 carrots and cook in the soup 30 minutes before dinner time. The vegetables should hold their shape and be slightly crisp.

While the soup is simmering, make some baking powder dumplings and drop them in for the last 30 minutes with the potatoes and carrots.

Mix dry ingredients and add sour cream. Form little balls for dumplings. If batter is too dry, add a little water. Drop into boiling soup, lower heat, and let simmer for 30 minutes.

Dumplings

>   1 cup sour cream
> 1½ cups flour
>   2 tsp. baking powder
>   1 tsp. baking soda

Parsley Scallops

Rinse scallops and pat dry. Place in a paper bag filled with flour. Shake until all are well-coated. Place scallops on a board or plate. Cut in half or quarters with scissors, unless the scallops are extremely small. Make sure all excess flour is removed. Put butter and oil in a large frying pan; heat until it sizzles and then throw in the·

> 1-1½ lbs. scallops [450 - 680 g]
>   enough flour to coat
>   scallops
>   2 tbsp. butter and 2 tbsp.
>   oil [more if necessary]

43

½ bunch parsley, finely
  chopped
  salt, pepper, lemons
2 cloves garlic, crushed
  [or more]

scallops. Cook on moderate heat from 5 to 10 minutes or until they begin to brown.

Add ½ bunch of chopped parsley and the garlic; stir scallops, parsley and garlic for about 2 minutes. Serve immediately with lemon wedges. Serves 4.

(An easy way to chop parsley is with the blender. Fill the blender ⅓ full of water. Tear ½ bunch of parsley frizz into 2 or 3 parts. Place in blender and buzz several seconds. Drain water from parsley in a strainer. Your parsley will be expertly chopped.)

Salmon Cooked in Foilwrap

5 or 6 lb. salmon
[2.25 kg to 2.75 kg]
fresh dill [a whole bunch]
salt
freshly ground pepper
lemon slices
bay leaf
about ¼ cup butter

Place the salmon on heavy-duty foilwrap. Arrange everything else under or on top of salmon. Dot with butter. Seal foilwrap so that no juices can seep out. Bake in 350° F (175° C) for 40 minutes or until the thickest part of the fish is flaky. Plunge a skewer into fish; if it flakes right through, the fish is right.

Serve hot, with the juices in the foil poured over it, along with extra lemon and melted butter. If you wish to serve it cold, let the fish cool before removing it from the foil.

44

How to Boil Live Lobster

Put the live lobster in some salted water — sea water if possible — bring to a boil and let it cook twelve minutes, sixteen if you're worried (lobsters lose their tenderness if overcooked). Then cool it off slightly under fresh, cold water. Crack and eat it.

Green Tomato Relish

Spread the tomatoes (sliced) in layers on a large, deep platter, sprinkling each layer with salt, using ¼ cup of salt in all. Cover platter and let it sit for a few hours at room temperature. Drain liquid that has accumulated around the tomatoes and transfer them to a 6-quart (6.8 l) enamel casserole. Add the onions, peppers, sugar, celery seed, mustard, cinnamon, allspice, cloves and the remaining salt. Pour in the vinegar; it should cover the vegetables completely. Bring mixture to a boil and simmer, partially covered, for 5 minutes or until the vegetables are barely tender. Ladle the relish at once into hot, sterilized jars. Makes 120 oz. (3.4 l).

about 6 lbs. [2.75 kg] firm green tomatoes, stemmed, cut in half and then cut cross wise into ½ inch [1.25 cm] thick slices
½ cup salt
2 lbs. [907 g] onions, peeled and cut crosswise into thin slices
8 medium-sweet red peppers, seeded and cut into strips
1 cup brown sugar
2 tsp. dry mustard
6 whole cloves
2 tsp. celery seed
2 tsp. ground cinnamon
1 tsp. allspice
3-5 cups vinegar

5. Quebec and the Pork Question

"French Canadians — they eat pork," the important gentleman from Montreal said, disdainfully. The gentleman was not French Canadian but a descendant of early Scotch settlers in Quebec. "Pigs are easier to raise than cows, that's why they eat a lot of pork," he reiterated.

This gentleman didn't realize that every group in Canada with a rural heritage, like the Ukrainians, the Germans, Irish and especially the Scotch prized the pig for the same reason. (Many towns and counties settled by the Scotch honor the place where the sows used to forage for their litter by calling it Hog Road or Hog St. John Kenneth Galbraith, in his book, The Scotch, says that in Dunwich Township, Ontario, Hog was changed to Hogg St. because there was a desire to combine authenticity with elegance.)

Fèves au lard, rôti du porc, ragoût de pattes, and tourtière are definitely French Canadian dishes. Yet what person of English or Scotch background finds pork and beans, roast pork and pork pie unusual to eat? It's not so much what French Canadians eat, it's how they make it that counts. French Canadians believe that cooking and eating are important occupations. The English and French are our "founding nations," but it is only the French who can claim the heritage of truly loving and respecting food. Local Quebec recipe books print ten different ways of making tourtière and beignes (doughnuts), and grand-pères (dumplings cooked in maple syrup). According to many Quebecois the best cooks in the province come from Lac St. Jean or near the Saguenay in Eastern Quebec, where les perles bleues du Saguenay, les gourganes, and l'ouananiche flourish — blueberries, lentils, and small river salmon. Mme. Benoit refers to the district in her Canadian cookbook, and Mme. Cécile Roland has published a cookbook with recipes by the local people. If you ask an Ontarian, "Where do the best cooks come from in your province?" you'd get a blank look. Someone might mutter "Kitchener-Waterloo county," but the flourishing Mennonite cooking tradition has been limited to that area.

French Canadians have been leaving their farms and fishing villages for the past one hundred years and the average French Canadian now is urban rather than rural. The two best cities in Canada for restaurants are without a doubt Montreal and Quebec City, and Quebec City has a population of about five hundred thousand, smaller than Hamilton (not exactly a gastronomic Valhalla). Many fin becs, or gourmets, swear that Quebec is even better than Montreal, not because Quebec is a rich town, but because the locals have always loved good cooking and know enough about food to frequent restaurants that keep up standards. The number of good restaurants in Quebec per capita is unequalled anywhere in Canada, perhaps North America. Until recently most restaurants in Quebec City and Montreal did not serve traditional country food like ragoût de pattes, tourtière and sugar pie. Sophisticated urban cuisine — coq au vin, meringue Chantilly, and Chateaubriand — was their mainstay.

These dishes have their roots in France. And the educated upper-class French Canadians who taught their servants to cook from recipe books printed in France during the nineteenth century, now expect these dishes at restaurants during the twentieth century. French cooking, or as they say in English Canada "Parisian cooking," is just as much a part of French Canada as fève au lard and maple syrup. French Canadians were eating escargot in restaurants and at home decades before the first brave Torontonian took his first garlicky forkful.

Elaborate French cuisine rather than simple Quebec cooking has been the tradition and, to a great extent, still is in Quebec restaurants. But when the wave of nationalism came over the province some fifteen years ago, smart restaurateurs appealed to the emotions as well as the pocketbooks of French Canadians and began to serve tourtière, and sugar pies, previously disdained by restaurant owners and clients alike. Just outside Quebec City on l'Ile d'Orléans, L'Atre, a thriving restaurant, serves tourtière and sugar pie in an eighteenth century Quebec farmhouse lit by gaslight. The sugar pie is made of real maple sugar, and the cream you drench it with is the thickest I've tasted this side of Devonshire. It's real farmers' cream, the crème de la crème.

People in Quebec are so interested in good food that there are thirty-three officially registered dining clubs in the province and countless private dining or wine-tasting clubs. I attended four of them, and the menus offered dishes like Oysters Rockefeller, filet of sole cardinale, sweetbreads in Noilly Prat, and Veuve Cliquot 66 Champagne. The members were lawyers, engineers, insurance agents, Liberals, Conservatives and Separatists. They all criticized the chef if a certain dish was not up to their standards. One man even graded each item from A- to C+, filing away the marks for future reference. And when the chef would take a digestif with the guests, he'd hear, "I do think the tournedos were a little overcooked." To these Quebecois, who are not untypical, good food is worth any price, and they often pay $75 a person for the pleasure of eating it.

At Christmas French Canadians often combine the two gastronomic threads, rural and the sophisticated urban, in one meal like André Ouellette's reveillon. André and his wife, Francine, both work in Ottawa, but are Montreal born and bred. André, the son of a fireman, reminisced, "At Christmas, when I was little, I always wished for an electric train and got mittens instead." Francine, on the other hand, comes from a wealthier family, and remembers getting art books and encyclopedias from an uncle who was a Monseigneur, and eating Italian meringues and babas au rhum ordered from a fancy bakery. But they both ate traditional food at the reveillon — tourtière, cretons (pork paté), beignes and bûches de Noël.

Their meal in Ottawa reflected the two kinds of cooking that goes on in Quebec. We ate tourtière and cretons, courtesy of Francine's aunt, and then we went on to artichokes vinaigrette, coq au vin, salad and imported cheese. We drank Veuve Cliquot 66 with André's specialty, crêpes suzettes flambées. André had thought of making a bûche de Noël for the reveillon, but he wasn't quite sure how you get the cake all rolled up like a carpet — "That always has been a great mystery to me." Francine refused to show him how because the dessert was his job. Being a fireman's son, he felt that a few flames singeing his eyebrows would not be amiss, and settled on crêpes flambées.

SOME TRADITIONAL QUEBEC COUNTRY RECIPES.

Why not start off with pork, like the gentleman said.

Rôti du Porc with Sugar and Vinegar

Place the roast on broiler rack and pin onion slices on with toothpicks. Stick on cloves. Roast uncovered at 400°F (205°C) for 3 hours. During the last half hour, baste with a glaze made with sugar, cornstarch and vinegar, boiled until it thickens. (This is a version of a recipe from **A French Canadian Cook Book** by Donald Asselin.)

1 lb. loin of pork [454 g]
2 sliced Spanish onions to pin on the roast
1 tbsp. cloves [whole]
½ cup brown sugar
2 tsp. cornstarch
¼ cup vinegar

Navarin of Lamb in Quebec Cider

Quebec produces an excellent cider that may be bought at groceries and the liquor commission. It's alcoholic and comes dry, medium and sweet. Use the cider that suits your taste; I prefer the dry.

Dredge the meat with flour and brown in fat or oil, for 2 or 3 minutes. Add seasonings, garlic, potato, turnips and onions. Add cider and simmer for 1 hour or 1 hour and 15 minutes. Correct seasoning and serve.

4 lbs. of lamb shoulder or loin, cut into cubes [1.8 kg]
1 tsp. nutmeg
1 tsp. thyme
2 large chopped onions
2 cups diced potatoes
1 cup diced turnips
4 tbsp. oil, or bacon fat
3 tbsp. flour
3 cups cider
2 cloves garlic [optional]

André's Coq au Vin

½ lb. salt pork cut into small
    cubes [227 g]
1 tbsp. butter
12 to 16 small white onions, left
    whole and peeled [if these are
    not available, cut up 3
    medium onions in 6 pieces]
3 to 4 lb. frying chicken, cut in
    8 pieces [1.35 kg to 1.8 kg]
    cooking oil, if necessary
¼ cup of brandy, or whiskey
2 to 3 cups red wine
2 bay leaves
    several sprigs of parsley and
½ cup of chopped celery tops
2 to 3 tbsp. flour
1 tsp. thyme
    salt and pepper to taste
2 tbsp. butter
½ lb. mushrooms [227 g]
1 tsp. chopped garlic
2 tbsp. chopped parsley
1 tbsp. tomato paste

Blanch salt pork in a little boiling water and drain. Sauté salt pork in the tablespoon of butter until crisp. Remove and set them aside. Brown onions in the rendered fat and remove them when they are golden. Set them aside. Dredge chicken in flour and add some oil to the fry pan. When the oil is smoking add chicken and brown pieces on both sides. Turn off heat. Heat brandy in a small sauce pan and set it on fire with a long match. Pour flaming brandy over chicken. When the brandy flame has died down add wine, herbs and mushrooms. Cook for 30 minutes, or until wine has reduced so it just covers the chicken. Add tomato paste, butter. Cook 10 minutes more. Add onions, parsley and pork fat. Simmer until everything is hot. Season to taste. (May be made the day before.) Serves 4 to 6.

Whitefish or Salmon (Ouananiche) with Rice and Lemon Stuffing

Sauté vegetables in butter and mix with rest of ingredients.

Stuff fish with this mixture. Wrap fish in foil and bake 30 to 40 minutes at 350° F (175° C). (A version of stuffed whitefish from **A French Canadian Cook Book**)

4 to 6 lb. fish [1.8 kg to 2.7 kg]
1 cup chopped celery
2 cups chopped onions
⅓ cup butter
¼ lb. raw chopped mushrooms [113 g]
1 cup water
½ to ¾ cup lemon juice
1½ cups cooked rice
1 tbsp. of grated lemon rind
¼ tsp. thyme
salt and pepper to taste

Maple Rice Pudding

a nice homely recipe

Mix together and pour into 8″ pan (20.3 cm). Set in another pan of hot water. Bake for 45 minutes at 350° F (175° C).

1 cup rice
3 beaten eggs
½ cup raisins
2 cups milk
1 cup maple syrup

Le Bouilli de Quebec

A most traditional recipe and wonderful for 10 to 12 people. The best I ever ate was Anita Cadieux's; she made it in her summer cottage. Anita is the wife of one of Canada's senior diplomats, Marcel Cadieux.

3 or 4 qts. water [4.55 l]
4 lb. stewing chicken
   [1.8 kg]
3 to 4 lbs. short ribs or blade
   steak [1.35 kg to 1.8 kg]
1 lb. salt pork, as lean as
   possible [454 g]
2 tsp. coarse salt
1 tsp. nutmeg
1 tsp. savory
12 leeks or small onions
12 carrots, scraped
12 new potatoes
4 stalks celery
2 lbs. yellow or green beans
   [907 g]
   freshly ground pepper

Remove all fat from chicken. Cut in 8 pieces and place in the largest pot you have. Add meat, salt pork, and salt. Cover with water. Add nutmeg and thyme or savory. Simmer for about 2 hours or until meat and chicken are tender. Add leeks or onions, carrots, potatoes and celery. Cook for 15 minutes and add beans. Simmer until beans are cooked but not overdone. Season. To serve, place meat and chicken and vegetables on a platter and eat it with horseradish or a vinaigrette sauce.

Fèves au Lard

1 large onion stuck with 2
   cloves
2 lbs. salt pork, blanched and
   cut in cubes [907 g]
3 cloves garlic
1 tbsp. dry mustard
½ cup molasses
   salt and pepper to taste

Soak one quart (1.15 l) of navy or pea beans in water overnight. Drain beans.

Cover beans with water, add onion, salt pork, garlic, mustard and molasses. Let mixture cook 3 to 4 hours until liquid is just about absorbed and beans are mushy. Add extra water if needed.

Grand-Pères au Sirop d'Erable

dumplings in maple syrup

Combine dry ingredients in a bowl. Cut in butter as for pie dough and pour in milk. Stir until batter is smooth. In a deep casserole or pot bring the water and syrup to a boil. Stir well. Drop the batter in syrup by the heaping tablespoon, spacing them 1 to 2 inches apart. Reduce heat, cover tightly and simmer for 15 minutes. When done the dumplings should be puffed and dry inside. Let the dumplings cool to lukewarm before serving.

1½ **cups flour**
2 **tsp. baking powder**
2½ **tbsp. chilled butter**
¼ **cup milk**
2 **cups maple syrup**
½ **cup water**

Cretons

Cretons, or **grattons**, is a sort of meat spread made from pork that is simmered for a very long time with onions and various spices, including cinnamon. It solidifies when cold and makes a very good filling for sandwiches, or a cracker spread. Cretons is so popular among French Canadians that big companies like Belle Fermière make their own commercial brand and sell it on supermarket counters. However, if you want to regulate the amount of fat you're eating, you can easily make a leaner variety yourself. Some recipes call for melting down 4 pounds (1.8 kg) of leaf lard, but this amount would do horrendous things to your cholesterol count. It's not necessary to use so much fat. Take a pound or so of ordinary ground pork (454 g) (if the butcher is nice, ask him to give a second grinding) and place it in a saucepan with two chopped onions, garlic, a teaspoon of cinnamon,

dry mustard and sage or thyme, perhaps a ground raw carrot, enough water to cover very slightly, and a piece of salt pork. Simmer for one and one half to two hours, adding more water to prevent burning. You will have a good meat spread that is solid when cooled but not too fatty.

Tourtière with Tomato

Pastry

2¼ cups flour
  2 ice-cream scoops or 2 heaping tbsps. shortening
  1 tsp. thyme
  ¼ lb. butter [113 g]
  1 egg
    a little cold water

Combine as for pie crust; makes top and bottom crust.

Filling

  ¾ lb. ground beef [340 g]
  ¾ lb. ground pork [340 g]
  ¼ lb. salt pork, cut into cubes [113 g]
  3 cooked potatoes, cut into cubes
  1 14 oz. can tomatoes [397 g]
  3 onions sliced
    garlic, ginger and cinnamon, 1 tsp. of each

Put salt pork in good-size frying pan. Let it cook about 6 minutes and then add garlic, onions and meat. Stir well and cook 5 more minutes. Add tomatoes, potatoes and spices. Simmer for ¾ of a hour. Let it cool, and then place on top of rolled-out bottom crust. Cover with remaining crust and bake in oven for 45 minutes at 350° F (175° C). (You may make this in advance and freeze it before baking.)

All quantities given are approximate. There is no reason why you may not have more or less pork or beef or onions.

Ragoût des Boulettes

Brown the pork hocks and then add the onions and water. In the meantime, combine the ground veal, ground pork or beef, spices and parsley. Take 2 slices of bread; soak them in water and squeeze them through your fingers to form a paste; add to the meat mixture along with the raw eggs. Shape into meatballs. Place the meatballs on top of the simmering hocks and onions and allow to cook about 20 minutes.

Make a paste of browned flour and a little milk or water and add it to the stew. If you don't have a box of browned flour and you don't feel like browning a little over a frying pan yourself, add some instant-blending flour to the stew.

It's best to cook the ragoût the day before you plan to eat it so you will have a chance to skim off the fat after it cools. The pork hocks and spices give this family supper dish a certain distinction.

2 pork hocks
1 lb. hamburger or ground pork [454 g]
2 Spanish onions, chopped
2 cups water
1 or 2 eggs
  cinnamon and garlic
  salt and pepper to taste
1 lb. ground veal [454 g]
  browned flour or instant-blending flour
  ginger
  parsley
  cloves
2 slices bread

Veau dans le Chaudron

I was given this recipe by Mme. Anita Cadieux.

Veal must be juicy and flavorful; too often it is treated as pork and cooked far too long. The secret is the retention of juices, which makes this roast veal a new eating experience.

6 to 7 lb. roast of veal, preferably the rump [3.17 kg]
1 medium-sized red cabbage
2 apples
2 large Spanish onions
1 large clove of garlic
   salt and crushed pepper
4 cloves
1 cup or more, cider or beer
1 cup of chicken or beef stock
2 or 3 slices fresh side pork

Set oven at 350° F (175° C). A heavy cast-iron casserole or covered roaster should be used.

Slice the cabbage, onions and apples. Mix together, along with garlic and cloves and lots of crushed pepper. Place the vegetable-and-apple mixture on the bottom of the roaster. Pour the beer or cider and stock over it. (If you are using beer, add a few more apples.) Set veal on top of cabbage; salt and drape the side-pork slices over veal.

Cover the meat with foilwrap and then place the lid on the roaster. Roast 1½ to 2 hours with lid and foil always in place. The cabbage will still be crunchy and the meat will be full of juice.

Cipaille

A Lac St. Jean Specialty

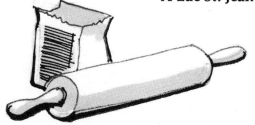

Cipaille, sipaille or cipâte is a pie made with 5 layers (cinq pâtés). In the old days the meat filling was always game. This is an urban no-game version of a traditional dish.

Pastry
   4 cups flour
   6 tsp. butter
   6 tsp. shortening
   1 tsp. salt
   4 tsp. baking powder
   ½ cup cold water
   ¼ cup milk

Blend as for pie crust dough, adding liquid last. Refrigerate until ready to use. Then, divide dough into 3, 4 or 5 sections, depending on the height of your casserole, and roll out each section, making one section larger than the rest (I use 3, because my cast-iron container is 4 inches (10 cm) deep and will only take 3 layers).

The instructions that follow refer to the ingredients as I was able to obtain them. If you happen to have access to fresh fowl and game, you should of course alter the method accordingly. For example, if you have tender partridges on hand, and young hare, the meat should be just browned and then stripped from the bones in large pieces. The full cooking should take place in the pie.

With a frozen fowl, I compromise by throwing it into a pot and simmering it, along with pork hocks, gizzards, salt, pepper, cloves and bay leaves, for 3 to 4 hours — or until the meat falls off the bone easily. (At this stage, taste and adjust seasoning accordingly.) About 15 minutes before this chicken stock is ready, add parsnips, carrots and ½ bunch parsley, including the stalks. Throw in the 3 potatoes any time you like but remember to take them out when they're still firm. Let them cool and then grate.

While the chicken is boiling and the duck defrosting, put a good chunk of butter and some olive oil in a heavy-bottomed pan or casserole; when it sizzles, add the ground meat, chopped onions, celery, garlic, leek, some of the salt and pepper and thyme. Mix well, cover and simmer for about 40 minutes. When the ground mixture is cooked, add the grated potatoes and the rest of the parsley.

When the duck is defrosted, hack it in 3 or 4 chunks and sauté them lightly for about 5 minutes so that it will be easier to strip the meat from the bone. (Since the duck is more tender than the fowl, it doesn't need the long simmering.)

Filling

- 1 large boiling fowl
- 1 duck [if frozen, defrost in warm water]
- 3 pork hocks and/or calves feet
- 3 parsnips
- 3 large carrots
- 5 whole cloves
- 3 large potatoes
- 1 bunch parsley [chopped with stalks]
- 1 lb. ground pork [454 g]
- 1 lb. ground beef or veal [454 g]
- ½ lb. chicken livers, gizzards and hearts from duck and chicken [227 g]
- 3 large chopped onions
- 3 or 4 cloves garlic
- 1 leek [if possible] celery
- 3 tsp. salt cracked pepper
- 2 tsp. thyme
- 2 bay leaves
- 3 large dill pickles
- 1½ bottles of stuffed olives with pimentos [15 oz. bottle or 425 ml]

Take the largest piece of dough and line a casserole with it, bringing the sides up to the top if possible. Prick the dough with a fork. Spread olives and chopped pickles on it, then ground meat mixture, chicken, duck, and whole, raw livers and hearts. Add more seasoning if necessary. Add second layer of dough and repeat process. Seal with last layer.

Cut a hole in the center of the dough and, using a funnel, pour into the pie the stock in which the chicken cooked. Be sure all the layers get moistened. Replace the piece of dough cut to make the hole. Bake **cipaille** in 350° F (175° C) oven for 60 to 80 minutes. It may be eaten hot or cold.

Crème Caramel

1¼ cups sugar
¾ cup water

Heat the sugar over a low fire, preferably in a wide, flat pan, until it turns brown. Then slowly pour in the water. Boil until sugar is dissolved and the water brown.

Custard
1 cup cream
1 cup milk
1 tbsp. vanilla
3 eggs
½ cup sugar

Combine, and then scald, cream and milk. Beat together 3 egg whites, 2 egg yolks, and ½ cup sugar until frothy. Add vanilla to milk mixture and gradually pour it into eggs, stirring constantly.

Pour caramel (the sugar and water mixture) into a ring mold and swish it around until the inside of the mold is well-coated. Pour the custard into the mold and set it in a pan of hot water. Bake in a moderate oven for 45 minutes or until a knife inserted comes out clean. Unmold when cold. Serves 6.

Although classical **crème caramel** has always been part of French-Canadian upper-class cuisine, a more regional version exists: Take a can of Eagle Brand sweetened condensed milk, put it in simmering water for four hours and then open it up. A brown syrupy caramel milk will have formed. This was a real Christmas treat for a friend of mine. Since it's cloying, it's best eaten as a sauce for a cake or ice cream.

Layered Maple Pie even better than sugar pie

Cut butter into sifted flour; add egg and sour cream. You may refrigerate the dough or use it immediately. Divide dough into 2 balls and roll out the first as thin as possible so that you can get oblong pieces from it. Each should cover the length of an oblong Pyrex dish. Prick the 2 pieces of dough with a fork and lay 1 piece on the bottom.

If your maple sugar is already granulated, spread some over the dough. If it is in a big block, grate it first. Pour some unwhipped cream over the sugar. Place the other piece of dough on top of the cream and sugar.

Repeat the process with the next ball of dough. You should get 2 more pieces of dough, each pricked with a fork. Cover the whole dish with the last piece and seal it well. Try to keep the cream within the 3 layers; it shouldn't seep to the top. Bake in a 400° F (205° C) oven for about 30

20 oz. cream [unwhipped]
[568 ml]
1 lb. maple sugar [454 g]
my special sour-cream dough
or a rich pie crust dough

Sour-Cream Dough

2 cups flour sifted with 2 tsp. baking powder
¼ cup butter
½ - ⅔ cup sour cream
1 beaten egg

59

to 40 minutes. Watch it during the later stages so that it doesn't brown too much.

Let it cool, and slice into oozing squares. This dessert thumbs its nose at all doctors and dentists.

Maple Sugar Mousse

2 pkgs. gelatin, softened in
   ½-¾ cup strong coffee
7 eggs, separated
2 tsp. cornstarch
1 cup maple sugar [granulated]
1½ cups boiling milk
½ cup whipping cream
   salt
1 tbsp. sugar

Beat egg yolks. Add sugar and cornstarch slowly. Continue beating for about 3 minutes. Beat milk into eggs and sugar mixture. Stir with wooden spoon over low heat. Do not boil. Custard should thicken enough to coat spoon. Add gelatin and beat in until thoroughly dissolved.

Beat egg whites, adding a pinch of salt and 1 tbsp. sugar, until soft peaks form; then carefully fold whites into warm custard. Place in refrigerator until mixture is cold but not set. It may be necessary to fold the cooling mixture again in case it separates.

Whip ½ cup whipping cream and add to mousse. Turn the mousse into an 8-cup mold. Chill for 4 to 5 hours or overnight. Unmold and decorate with caramelized maple sugar.

6. Tortellini and the Di Ceccos

Tortellini is a specialty of an area in Northern Italy called Romagna, which encompasses Bologna. Like ravioli, tortellini is a meat and cheese stuffed envelope of pasta, but it's small and ring shaped, and looks like a belly button. A 17th century Bolognese story maintains that tortellini was born when a chef molded his pasta in the navel of a beautiful woman. (From all accounts this arduous method of making tortellini has become extinct, even in parts of Romagna where labor-saving devices are least prevalent.) Nevertheless, tortellini is still handmade, by skilled cooks.

Mrs. Salvatore Di Cecco lives in Richmond Hill outside of Toronto with her husband, who has retired from the macaroni and restaurant business. Mrs. Di Cecco was born in Romagna and is expert at making tortellini. Christmas, 1973, she used 170 eggs in the pasta and distributed tortellini and other pasta specialties to friends and relatives. But Mr. Di Cecco is not so keen on tortellini. In Italy during the war, "when one piece of beef was like an emerald," he traded a large amount of macaroni for some cheese, eggs, and meat. His wife, though only eighteen , knew how to make tortellini. There was tortellini all over the kitchen, dotting every sofa and chair in the living room, and spread on every bed in the house. They ate tortellini for weeks. Mr. Di Cecco said, "People were dying of everything in Italy, at that time, but I was the only person who nearly died of tortellini."

Mr. Di Cecco is a bit rueful about his wife's expertise at making noodles. "My family has been in the macaroni business for one hundred and fifty years, but what can I do, she insists on making her own pasta." It's like Mrs. Heinz offering her homemade chili sauce instead of ketchup with the hamburgers. Not that Mr. Di Cecco doesn't adore his wife's cooking. "Would you believe that I was one hundred and twenty pounds when I married?" He sighed, looking down at his waistline, which has spread some since he was a groom.

When the Di Ceccos came to Canada twelve years ago, they were astonished by what Canadians considered Italian food. Once at a restaurant, they were presented with two large balls with the spaghetti. They had never eaten spaghetti with meatballs before in their life. Mr. Di Cecco despairs every time he sees a Beeferoni or canned ravioli commercial on the T.V. "They call it Italian style, but their so-called Italian style just ruins the taste for real Italian food."

Mr. Di Cecco came over from Italy to manage the Romi macaroni factory. Mrs. Di Cecco can test the keeping qualities of the macaroni just by touching the dough, (macaroni must reach a certain degree of dryness in order for it to last without breaking or going moldy), and if you set forty kinds of wheat in front of Mr. Di Cecco he will tell you what kind of pasta to make from each variety.

Mrs. Di Cecco comes from the part of Italy where pasta contains eggs, whether ring-shaped like tortellini, ribbon-shaped, like tagliatelle, or fine as a string on a mandolin, like a capellini. (The southern part of Italy is poorer, and its pasta usually is made without eggs.) Ragù, or meat sauce, made from a blend of chopped veal, pork, butter, carrots and onions, is a Bolognese specialty, while the cheaper tomato sauce is often called Neapolitan.

Most Italians in Canada come from the south, Calabria, near the tip of the boot, and Sicily. Toronto has almost 300,000 of the 740,000 people of Italian extraction. The biggest emigration started after 1951. Since that time, shops selling blocks of Parmesan cheese, with bins of olives, and vegetables like artichokes, egg plant, and zucchini, (until then ignored by most Canadians), have become commonplace. Even the big supermarkets in the districts with a large Italian community, sell pasta machines, and rappini (sort of a butter spinach). Canada's palate has become educated despite pizza, canned ravioli and meatballs. Restaurants in Toronto, Montreal and Vancouver serve lasagna, canneloni, and even saltimbocca (slices of ham, veal and sage, tied together and sautéed in butter and wine) to eager Canadians who don't blink an eye at the names on the menu or sniff fearfully for the aroma of garlic.

My first experience eating Italian food was in 1955 on the Cristoforo

Colombo, then the flagship of the Italian line, which sailed from New York to Naples. Every evening, I would put on a pink peau de soie dress and come down for dinner, and every evening I would order the same dish, Noodles Alfredo. The headwaiter would light a chafing dish, place the noodles made from the chef's own pasta and cooked **al dente**, in the dish, and raise the strands high in the air, mixing them with half a pound of sweet butter and a small amount of freshly grated Parmigiano, as well as an unmeasured amount of warmed thick cream. Gently he would ladle half the noodles from the chafing dish onto my plate, and place the pepper grinder in front of me. As I leaned over for my first forkful, the napkin invariably fell off my lap, (linen never stays put on silk), and seven waiters would rush to pick it up. I was on the boat twelve days; by the time we were halfway through the voyage, everybody in the dining room would wait for the moment when the girl in the pink dress leaned over her noodles. The waiters treated the napkin-drop as signal for a kind of conversation; their English was nearly as bad as my Italian. "You like Italian food," they'd say, "Italian men good too." I'd murmur, "Lovely noodles, lovely noodles," too shy for anything else.

Canneloni

Mrs. Di Cecco makes a tender canneloni, filled with meat, spinach, and cheese. She describes herself as a-pinch-of-this and a-handful-of-that kind of cook. She gave me her ingredients but was a little hazy about the measurements.

Pasta

1 lb. flour, a little more if necessary [454 g]
5 medium eggs
8 quarts of boiling water [9 l]
10 quarts U.S.
1 tbsp. salt

The secret of good canneloni, or for that matter, any pasta, is a homemade dough, which almost melts in with the stuffing, because it's so light.

Pour flour into a large mixing bowl. Make a well in the center, and break in eggs. Mix with your hands or a fork, until the dough can be shaped in a ball. Keep kneading, adding a little more flour if dough is too sticky to handle. When dough is shiny and elastic, divide into two, and roll out one ball until it is as thin as possible. Cut into rectangles of 2" by 3" (5 cm x 7.6 cm). Repeat with second ball.

Drop pasta into water, little by little, making sure they don't stick to the pot or each other. Return water to a boil and cook pasta for 5 minutes. Drain, cool, and lay pasta on paper towels to dry.

Crêpe Dough for Mock Canneloni

3 eggs
1 cup milk
½ tsp. salt
⅓ cup water
   not quite one cup
   of sifted flour

To get this dough absolutely right, you need years of experience, especially in Northern Italy. You can make a crêpe batter for canneloni with Mrs. Di Cecco's filling. It tastes almost as good.

Combine in a blender. Make sure all the lumps are gone. Melt 1 tbsp. of butter in an 8" (20 cm) fry pan. When the foam subsides, ladle enough batter to cover bottom of pan thinly. Tilt pan from side to side to spread evenly. Cook until lightly browned on one side. Remove crêpe from pan with browned side facing up. Cool and add a tablespoon of filling, flatten it, spread it over crêpe and roll like a carpet. When all the crêpes are stuffed, pour Mrs. Di Cecco's besciamella over them, and sprinkle the surface with grated Gruyère cheese. Or just use her tomato sauce and sprinkle that with cheese.

Brown in oven for 20 minutes.

Filling

[use half this recipe for the crêpe dough]

3 lbs. fresh spinach [cooked, chopped and drained] [1.36 kg]
½ lb. Ricotta or cream cheese [227 g]
½ lb. grated Parmesan cheese [227 g]
¼ lb. grated Romano cheese [113 g]
¼ lb. Gruyère cheese [113 g]
1 cup leftover beef or chicken or cooked minced beef
   a little grated lemon peel, and nutmeg to taste

Sauté spinach in butter. Mix all ingredients together, and place a tablespoon of filling in the bottom third of each pasta rectangle. Roll up like a carpet.

Mrs. Di Cecco covers and bakes her canneloni with a besciamella (white sauce) or a simple tomato sauce.

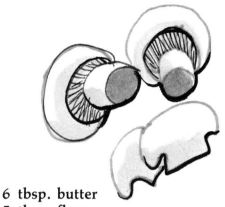

Besciamella

Melt butter in a heavy saucepan. When it is bubbling but not brown, add flour, little by little, until it's blended with butter. Pour in liquid and whisk and stir, until lumps have disappeared. Add mushrooms. Reduce heat when sauce begins to boil. Add salt, pepper and lemon juice when mixture is smooth and cooked.

Pour sauce over canneloni, and sprinkle a little Parmesan over the top. Bake for about 20 minutes at 300° F. (150° C) or until the canneloni is nicely browned on top.

6 tbsp. butter
5 tbsp. flour
1 cup milk
1 cup light cream
   salt, pepper, and a squeeze of lemon juice
1 lb. mushrooms with large caps [sometimes called steak mushrooms] chopped [454 g]
   a little grated Parmesan or Gruyère cheese

Mrs. Di Cecco's Tomato Sauce

Every August Mrs. Di Cecco goes to the market and buys a bushel of tomatoes. She makes her own tomato sauce and uses it during the winter over the pasta.

Combine everything except butter in a large pot, and simmer for 6½ hours. Add butter and cook ½ hour more. Freeze in plastic containers.

1 bushel tomatoes
3 tbsp. basil, chopped
8 carrots, chopped
4 onions, chopped
4 stalks celery, chopped
   salt, pepper to taste
½ pound butter [227 g]

65

Lasagne Pasta

2 scant cups flour
1 tbsp. salt
1 egg
1 small mashed potato
  enough lukewarm water to
  make a soft dough

Filling
½ lb. Gruyère cheese [227 g]
  Mrs. Di Cecco's full recipe
  for canneloni filling.

Mix flour, well-mashed potato, salt and egg. Add water for the soft dough. Let stand for one half hour. Roll dough until quite thin on floured board. For lasagne noodles cut into long rectangles. You can also make ravioli with this dough. For ravioli, cut into rectangles.

Use tomato sauce, and besciamella for alternate layers. Spread a large pan with ½ of spinach filling. Place ⅓ of lasagne pasta on top. Pour ½ white sauce over that, then ½ of the tomato sauce. Spread with spinach filling. Cover with pasta. Pour rest of tomato and white sauce over pasta. Place rest of pasta over sauce. Grate cheese over the surface. Bake for 25 minutes until top is nicely browned. May be prepared the day before.

Roast Chicken

Mrs. Di Cecco made the most delectable roast chicken I've ever tasted. She roasts it at a high temperature, 450° F (230° C) and bastes it every ten minutes with butter, oil and the juice from the chicken. It's done in about an hour.

Bagna Cauda

Literally "a hot bath"; you might call it an Italian fondue. It's perfect for a late night supper, or a hot dip at a buffet dinner. In Italy it's a first course. Italians know how to use vegetables; Bagna Cauda gives you the opportunity for tasting as many different vegetables as you like, with the fondue. Serve the vegetables raw.

Use a fondue dish or heavy enamelled saucepan to cook the Bagna Cauda in. Melt butter, but don't let it brown. Add anchovies, garlic and cream. Let sauce simmer, not boil, and keep stirring for 10 minutes. Simmer it another 10 minutes, giving it a stir, once in a while. If you are using a fondue dish, keep it on a low flame. Dip raw vegetables in sauce, using fingers or forks.

long strips of zucchini
carrots
celery
red or green pepper
Belgian endive, broken
into separate leaves
broccoli
4 cups cream
5 tbsp. butter
10 flat anchovy fillets, drained,
rinsed and chopped
1-2 tbsp. finely chopped garlic
lemon juice, salt, pepper to
taste

Pesto Sauce

Every summer I grow a lot of basil plants from seed. Basil is one of the easiest herbs to propagate, even in Ottawa where I live. If you have a black thumb, go to your local farmers' market where they sell bedding plants in the spring. More than likely you will find basil sold near the chives and parsley. I start making jars of pesto sauce when my basil plants are

67

flourishing in August. I clip the top leaves from several plants until I have about a cup. The plant benefits because it produces even more leaves after being pinched. Two weeks later the same plant will provide enough leaves for another jar of pesto. I must have made 8 last summer.

One Jar of Pesto
 1 cup fresh basil leaves
 ½ cup pignolia nuts or walnuts [optional]
    one or two cloves garlic
    juice ½ lemon
 ½ cup olive oil
 2 tbsp. freshly grated Parmesan cheese [optional]
    salt and pepper to taste

Place basil leaves, garlic, nuts, lemon juice in blender. Blend. Add oil slowly until you have a green purée. Mix in cheese and season. Pour pesto sauce in jars. This may be kept in the refrigerator for three weeks (at least) or frozen for several months. Add about two tablespoons of pesto sauce per serving of spaghetti or noodles **al dente.** Mix it well. More cheese may be added at the last moment.

Put a tablespoon of pesto sauce in a bowl of vegetable soup (homemade of course); the taste is marvellous.

Zucchini with Sicilian Sauce

 6 zucchini
 2 tbsp. butter
 1 tbsp. finely chopped green onions
 1 clove mashed garlic
 1½ tbsp. flour
 1 cup tomato juice
 4 anchovies
 ½ cup ripe black olives
 1 cup shredded mozzarella, or Gruyère cheese [I prefer Gruyère]

Parboil zucchini cut lengthwise, until tender but not mushy. While the vegetable is cooking, melt the butter in a saucepan and add green onions and garlic. Stir about 2 minutes. Don't brown. Sprinkle in flour, stirring hard, then add the tomato juice. Use a wire whisk to get rid of flour lumps. Simmer 5 minutes. Add anchovies, olives. Drain zucchini, and pour sauce over it. Sprinkle with grated cheese. Place under grill until cheese melts. Serve immediately.

Zucchini also goes well with pesto. Just cover with sauce and place under broiler.

Osso Buco

Allow 2 meaty veal shanks per person, approximately 1½" - 2" thick (5 cm) (if they are more than 2" (5 cm) thick, one shank each should be sufficient).

Season meat with salt and pepper and coat the pieces well with flour, shaking off the excess accumulation. Heat the olive oil in a large frying pan until it begins to smoke. Brown shanks on both sides, a few pieces at a time. Transfer them to a large platter.

Over a moderate heat melt the 4 tbsp. of butter in a large heavy-bottomed casserole dish. Add the chopped onions, carrots, celery, leek and garlic, and cook slowly until the vegetables are lightly colored. Then arrange the pieces of veal upright on the vegetables, making sure the marrow won't fall out as they cook. You may put one shank on top of another as long as they are lying with the bone facing up. Add wine, stock, tomatoes, herbs and bay leaf. The liquid should come more than half way up the sides of the meat. (More stock or wine might be needed later.)

You may cook this on top of your stove or in a 350° F (175° C) oven. Simmer for 45 minutes to 1 hour. The veal may be served at this stage but it tastes better if you go to the trouble of glazing it. (The glazing may be done just before serving.)

veal shanks
salt and freshly ground pepper
enough flour to coat each shank
8 tbsp. olive oil
4 tbsp. butter
1 cup chopped onion
½ cup chopped carrot
½ cup chopped celery
1 large chopped leek [not absolutely necessary]
2 cloves chopped or pressed garlic
1½ cups dry white wine
1 cup chicken or beef stock [canned is all right]
1 tsp. dried thyme
½ tsp. dried basil
1 large can of Italian plum tomatoes, drained and chopped

Gremolata

2 tbsp. finely chopped garlic
2 tbsp. grated lemon rind
1 cup finely chopped parsley
[there is no law against increasing or decreasing the proportions of lemon rind and garlic]

This is to be sprinkled on **osso buco** just before it is eaten, but it should be prepared while the meat is cooking.

Glazing

Remove the **osso buco** from the casserole and place it in a large ovenproof dish that will hold all the veal shanks in one layer. If you have a lot of liquid in the casserole, boil it down until the flavor is very intense. Pour some of the liquid over the shanks and glaze them on the upper shelf of the oven for about 10 minutes, or until shiny. Remove from oven; pour more of the reduced sauce over it for moisture, but don't drown the veal. Serve from the hot dish with more sauce on the side, and serve the **gremolata** separately so that each guest can sprinkle on as much as he likes. Little coffee spoons are good for scooping out the marrow.

Osso buco may be prepared the day before serving. It should serve 6 to 8 people.

Zuccotto

This fantasy was made by Raffaella, Mrs. Di Cecco's daughter-in-law. Raffaella doesn't make her own pasta, because she gets all she wants from her mother-in-law. But she will spend a week-end cleaning 15 pounds of mussels for a shellfish stew. She also specializes in desserts, like this one which combines everything Italians love: ice cream, candied fruits, and liqueur-soaked cake. It's a dessert you'll never forget and not difficult to make.

Line a large buttered bowl with waxed paper; line bowl with the sponge cake. Mix nuts, chocolate and peel into whipped cream. Pour whipped cream mixture into bowl. Freeze. This is very easy to unmold because of the waxed paper lining.

Serves 8 - 10

1 tbsp. grated lemon or orange peel

½ cup almonds, toasted and chopped

¾ cup hazelnuts, toasted and chopped

5 cups whipping cream and

⅔ cup sugar, whipped together

5 squares bitter chocolate grated or broken into small pieces

1 lb. sponge cake or pound cake [454 g], cut into ½" slices [1.25 cm], sprinkled with 4 tbsp. brandy and 4 tbsp. any sweet liqueur

7. Mrs. Mikos and the Toronto Austro-Hungarian Empire

"Dorothy, please look at what's happening, your cigarette ash dropped in my mashed potato dough." Mrs. Mikos was annoyed with her daughter, although she tried not to show it because I was present. We were standing in her small kitchen in Etobicoke, a suburb of Toronto, watching Mrs. Mikos prepare Hungarian plum dumplings. Dorothy Thomas scooped out the cigarette ash and took her scolding with equanimity. Like many daughters whose mothers are good cooks, Dorothy was banished from the kitchen at an early age. As an adult she is allowed to remain — to watch rather than to do. Dorothy is a Toronto alderwoman, and her mother is proud of her, but she trusts Dorothy more in City Hall than in the kitchen.

It was a sunny morning in Toronto, and we were drinking Mrs. Mikos' homemade plum wine which tastes a little like vermouth. Mrs. Mikos balanced a sugar cube on top of a pitted fresh prune plum that rested on a piece of dough. The next step was to wrap the sugar cube and plum in its mashed potato dough overcoat; Dorothy began to work the dough around the plum. Mrs. Mikos was suspicious. "Are you sure there is a sugar cube in this one? Make sure there are no holes, or the filling will slip out when I boil it." Mrs. Mikos has spent all her life in kitchens. She treats her pots and pans with confidence and care, like old friends. When she put her pastry board in the cupboard she patted it and said, "Off you go for a little rest now." As soon as she uses a spoon she washes it and uses it again. "When my Dorothy is in the kitchen, there are too many spoons to wash afterwards."

Mrs. Mikos was born in Hungary during the time of the Austro-Hungarian Empire. She left her family farm when she was seventeen and went to cooking school in Budapest. For a while she worked as a cook for a rich family in the city, but in 1937 Albert Mikos, an old beau who had been in Canada several years, paid the necessary five hundred dollar guarantee to the Canadian government and brought her to Canada as his bride. Since that time Mrs. Mikos has been preparing strudel, schnecken, and schnitzel in her kitchen or helping her husband, a tailor, in the basement sewing room.

Mrs. Mikos comes from hardy stock. Her grandmother in Hungary always went barefoot until late autumn and died when she was eighty-six. "She didn't die of old age, but of a broken heart. The government took her farm away from her in 1945." Mrs. Mikos is an expert carpenter, plasterer and weaver. She went to the Black Creek Pioneer Festival, was disgusted with the girls' weaving. "Oh my God, it was so lumpy; my grandmother would never let me get away with that."

When Mrs. Mikos was born, Hungary was part of the Hapsburg Empire which included Yugoslavia, Romania, Austria, Czechoslovakia, and a little bit of Poland. Through the centuries there was an intermingling of cooking styles. Yugoslavs, Poles, Hungarians, Czechs, Romanians and Austrians can all stake claim to dumplings, schnitzels, grilled meats, stews with cabbage, or sauerkraut, many-layered tortes and warm pancake desserts or "palatschinken." Of course there are strong regional differences. Hungarians use paprika and sour cream for their gulyas, Romanians eat mamaliga, (cornmeal mush), and Poles, like the Ukrainians and Russians, are mad about mushrooms, beet soups and meat-filled pastries. Yugoslavs (or rather, Serbs, Slovenians, Croatians, Montenegrins, and Macedonians) inherited an Oriental flavor to their cuisine from the old Turkish rule. They barbecue their meats and love sweets like halvah, (a Middle Eastern confection made from ground nuts, honey or sugar), and of course Turkish Delight.

Despite outraged denials from friends of Czech, Hungarian, and Polish descent, and of the other nations, their cooking styles have more similarities than contrasts, especially in Canada. Sources of primary ingredients are the same; Romanians, Poles, Czechs all go to Hungarian delicatessens for smoked meats and sausages, and they buy their veal and pork for schnitzels at Bittners, the German butcher. When I went to a restaurant called the Balkan Village in Toronto, I was served grilled lamb kebabs, (Yugoslavia), deep fried mushrooms,

(Poland), stuffed peppers, (Romania), and sugary lemon palatschinken, (Hungary and Czechoslovakia). Mrs. Mikos' Hungarian plum dumplings are unique in the sense that no one can make them with exactly the same flair — she's been cooking them for thirty years. But plum dumplings are a specialty of all the nations (except perhaps Yugoslavia) that formerly belonged to the Austro-Hungarian Empire.

I shall rename them "They Were Better the Last Time Plum Dumplings." Mrs. Mikos' husband says that, whenever he eats them, especially when there's company.

"They were better the last time" Plum Dumplings

Dough
  5 potatoes, cooked and
    squeezed through a ricer,
    or mixed with an electric
    beater
  1 large egg
  1 tsp. salt
  1 tbsp. oil
  1 tsp. baking soda
  1½ cups flour

Filling
a box sugar cubes
about 18 prune plums

Mix together with hands, very well, and let dough sit for an hour, covering it with the bowl.

Roll out dough as thin as possible without breaking it. Cut dough into rectangles. Place one whole split plum (with the pit removed) on each rectangle. Place a cube of sugar in the middle of the split plum.

Bring about 3 quarts (3.41 l) of salted water to a boil in a 4 quart (4.55 l) saucepan. Work dough around each plum, pinching and pleating, so there are no holes in the dough. With a large spoon, carefully place 4 of the dumplings in the water. Cover pan, leave water on high heat and cook for 6 or 7 minutes. Turn the dumplings over and let them boil about 5 minutes longer. Remove dumplings with a slotted spoon to paper towels to drain. Repeat process with other dumplings.

Topping

Mrs. Mikos browns some bread crumbs in a large fry pan with ¼ lb. of butter. She shakes the crumbs in the butter over a low heat until they are browned. Then she adds about two or three tablespoons of sugar to the browned butter mixture. The dumplings are shaken in the bread crumbs and sugar mixture until they are coated. You can keep the dumplings warm in the oven for an hour. These must be served warm. Pitted fresh apricots or damson plums are good substitutes. Above all, the dumplings must squirt when you take your first forkful.

Hungarian Chicken Paprika

Sauté chicken pieces in oil or lard until each side is browned, about 5 minutes for each side. Remove pieces as soon as they are browned and add raw ones to pan. Pour most of the fat from the frying pan. Add onions, garlic, salt and pepper and cook them for 8 minutes on a medium heat. Remove from heat to stir in paprika and mix well into the onions. Add chicken stock. Bring to a boil, stirring all the while. Return the chicken to pan, cover tightly. Bring liquid to a boil and let chicken cook for 20

3 or 4 pound chicken cut up [1.81 kg]
2 tbsp. lard, vegetable oil or vegetable oil and butter
2 cups of chopped onions
3 or 4 cloves garlic, smashed
2 tbsp. sweet Hungarian Paprika
3 to 4 cups chicken stock
2 cups sour cream
2 or 3 tbsp. flour
2 large green peppers chopped
3 tbsp. chopped dill [optional]
lemon juice, and salt
and pepper to taste

75

minutes. When the chicken is tender, remove to a platter.

Skim the fat off the liquid in the pan. Stir sour cream in a large bowl with flour, using a wire whisk. Add green peppers and dill to liquid and slowly stir in the sour cream and flour mixture. Simmer for 6 minutes. The sauce should be thick and smooth. Add chicken and its juices to sauce and re-heat for 3 or 4 minutes. Add salt, pepper and lemon juice to taste. (May be made the day before.)

Transylvanian Gulyas

1 lb. sauerkraut [fresh or canned] [454 g]
½ lb. chunk bacon, or salt pork cut into cubes [227 g]
1 cup chopped onions
2 lbs. pork loin, boned and cut into cubes [907 g]
2 tsp. caraway seeds
1 tsp. juniper berries
½ cup tomato purée
4-5 cups beef or chicken stock or water
1 cup sour cream
2 tbsp. flour
5 large potatoes

Wash sauerkraut, and soak in cold water for ½ hour to reduce the sourness.

Render bacon or salt pork and drain off most of the fat. Add onions to pan where the salt pork was rendered. Cook until lightly colored with pieces of salt pork. Add ½ cup of water or stock, bring to a boil, add cubed pork loins. Spread sauerkraut over pork and sprinkle caraway seeds and juniper berries over it. Add tomato purée and water or stock and cover. Bring pork, sauerkraut and liquid to a boil and simmer for 1 hour. Check to make sure liquid hasn't boiled away. If so, add some more.

When the pork is cooked, combine sour cream and flour in a bowl. Mix with a wire whisk. Carefully stir into the gulyas. About 40 minutes before the gulyas is cooked, cubed raw potatoes may be added, along with a little more liquid. Otherwise serve with egg noodles.

Macedonian Eggplant & Red and Green Pepper Caviar

Pierce eggplant with a fork in several places and bake in 350° F (175° C) oven for one hour, or until soft.

To roast the peppers, place a wire rack directly on the element of your stove. Heat element. Keep turning peppers on rack, a few at a time, until their skins pop, and all sides are charred. Remove stems and seeds, and peel peppers.

Peel eggplant and add to peppers while still hot. Add salt, garlic, vinegar and oil. Mash thoroughly, until you reach a texture that pleases you. Chill. Serve cold as an appetizer with bread.

1 eggplant
12 sweet peppers [red or green], washed and dried
4 cloves of garlic mashed
3 tbsp. of wine or cider vinegar
2 tbsp. salt
⅓ cup vegetable oil

Sugary Lemon Palatschinken

Beat the eggs with milk in a bowl, or blender. Combine with water. Stir or blend in flour and sugar. Add ¼ tsp. salt. Stir or blend until batter is smooth.

Melt 1 tsp. of butter in an 8″ (20 cm) fry pan. When the foam subsides, ladle in enough batter to cover bottom of pan thinly, and tilt pan from side to side, to spread evenly. Cook pancake

3 eggs
1 cup milk
⅓ cup water
   not quite one cup sifted flour
3 tbsp. sugar
¼ tsp. salt
   butter
   juice 1 large lemon
3 tbsp. icing sugar

77

until lightly browned and turn it over, until other side is browned. Continue until batter is gone. Mix two tablespoons of icing sugar and lemon juice together with a little butter. If mixture is too tart, add more icing sugar. Spread over pancakes. Roll pancakes up and sprinkle top with more icing sugar. Place pancakes in oven-proof dish and place in oven under grill for 3 or 4 minutes. Everything except the last step may be done the day before.

Palatschinken are delicious if you stuff them with cottage cheese and a few raisins instead of the lemon-sugar. Then you can serve them for supper to your children. Or why not mix the icing sugar with brandy instead of lemon and eat them yourself?

Czechoslovakian Sauerbraten

3 or 4 days beforehand

6 servings

  4 **lb. bottom round roast [1.8 kg]**
½ **cup pickling spices**
2½ **lemons**
  6 **slices bacon**
10 **sprigs fresh parsley**
  3 **ribs diced celery**
  2 **large carrots, chopped**
  2 **cups chopped onions**

Trim all fat from meat. Tie pickling spices in cheesecloth. Peel one lemon, and chop peel. Squeeze the juice from both lemons. Cook bacon in casserole. Remove bacon and use for something else. Add carrots, onions, celery and parsley to fat in casserole. Cook, stirring, until the vegetables are brown. Add pickling spices, lemon rind. Add enough boiling water to cover meat; let this mixture cool. Place meat in a deep glass or stainless steel dish and pour lemon juice and vegetable mixture over it. Cover and refrigerate for 3 or 4 days.

Day of Cooking

When ready to cook, pre-heat oven to 325° F (165° C). Remove meat from marinade but reserve vegetables and liquid. Salt and pepper meat, and brown meat in oil in a heavy casserole. Add 2 cups of liquid, salt and pepper, and cover. Bake, basting occasionally, for 2 hours. Add vegetables and more liquid if necessary. Continue baking 45 minutes more, or until meat is tender.

Remove cheesecloth bag. Remove meat and keep warm. Mash liquid and vegetables and bring to a simmer. Blend with cornstarch and water. Stir in sour cream and bring to a boil. Serve sauce over sliced meat.

3 tablespoons vegetable oil
2 tbsp. cornstarch
1 cup sour cream
½ cup water
  salt and pepper

Mrs. Mikos' Cold Water Schnecken

Mrs. Mikos showed me an old yellowed scribbler that she had brought from Hungary, thirty-seven years ago. These cold water schnecken were written in the scribbler, but the ink was faded and blurred. Mrs. Mikos has been cooking them by heart for many years. I found a similar recipe in a Manitoba Mennonite, a Jewish and an Austrian cookbook. Schnecken apparently follow the Danube into the Black Sea.

Schnecken are yeast buns that look like snails and should be eaten at least two at a time.

Soak yeast in ½ cup of warm water for about 10 minutes. Add egg yolks, cream, and butter to

1 pkg. yeast
4 egg yolks
¼ lb. butter [113 g]
5 oz. coffee cream [142 ml]
1 cup flour
  about 3 cups flour for kneading

yeast. Add flour and mix well. For kneading, add "as much flour as feels good" according to Mrs. Mikos and knead until the dough is soft, and integrated, not too long, about 2 or 3 minutes. Shape into a ball and put it into a cotton bag, old pillow-slip, or fasten a towel around it with safety pins. Mrs. Mikos puts it in the sink and lets cold water run over it for 4 hours. If dripping water annoys you, put it in a pail or large bowl of cold water, and let it sit, for 4 hours.

Sprinkle a board with some flour and lots of sugar and roll out the dough ¼ inch (6.25 mm) thick. The dough will be slightly sticky. Roll up as for jelly roll and cut in thin slices. Let them rise for another 40 minutes on a greased pan. Bake until they are golden in a 350° F (175° C) oven.

Romanian Mamaliga

Italians call it polenta, and a Scotsman might call it cornmeal porridge. It's best served with stews, or meat dishes with lots of gravy.

40 oz. water [1.14 l]
1 tbsp. salt
2½ cups yellow or white cornmeal
3 or 4 tbsp. melted butter

Bring salted water to a boil and add cornmeal, very slowly, stirring constantly with a wooden spoon. The water should not lose its boil. Reduce heat, cover, and cook for 10 minutes or until all the liquid has been absorbed. Pour melted butter over it and serve with meat course as a substitute for potatoes or rice.

Macedonian Halvah

I used to eat halvah when I went to the movies with a girlfriend in north Winnipeg. The grocery store next to the theatre was owned by Russian Jews who had huge blocks of it sitting on the counter. There were two flavors, chocolate and vanilla, and it was very rich. One day we bought thirty cents worth, which meant we each ate a pound, as we watched "The Secret Life of Walter Mitty." I never ate halvah after that for more than twenty years.

Melt butter in fry pan on medium heat; slowly mix in wheat hearts with a wooden spoon for 20 minutes or until mixture is golden brown. Boil sugar and water for 15 minutes. Pour syrup slowly into cooked wheat hearts, mixing continuously until all syrup is used. This mixture is very hot; be careful. Add walnuts, sesame seeds and cinnamon; if mixture seems too liquid boil another 5-7 minutes. Pour mixture into a mold and press into place.

Chill and turn out. Eat it as a dessert or a candy.

½ lb. butter [227 g]
¾ lb. farina or wheat hearts [340 g]
2½ cups sugar
3½ cups water
1 cup chopped walnuts
½ cup sesame seeds [toasted]
1 tsp. cinnamon

81

Czech Veal Steaks
with Anchovies and Ham

Lightly pound veal slices.

2 lbs. veal cutlets or steak [907 g]
¼ cup sweet butter
1 tbsp. anchovy paste
¼ lb. ham in slices [113 g]
2 eggs
¼ cup flour
1 cup bread crumbs
butter or lard for frying

Mix anchovy paste with sweet butter. Spread anchovy and butter mixture on each piece of veal. Place a slice of ham on paste side of veal slice. Flour both sides of veal, pressing ham well into the paste. Beat eggs. Dip veal slices in egg, then immediately in bread crumbs, coating both sides well. Let veal stand for ½ hour or so.

Melt butter or lard in pan till hot. Place veal slices in hot fat, ham side down, and fry on both sides till golden brown. Serve with noodles.

Chlodnik   Cold Beet Soup with Cucumbers and Shrimp
A hot day drink

4 cups buttermilk
1 cup sour cream
1½ cups diced, peeled, cooked beets
1 cup diced, peeled, seeded cucumbers
3 tbsp. minced green onions
¼ cup wine vinegar or lemon juice
¼ cup sugar
3 hardboiled eggs, chopped
½ lb. cooked shrimp [227 g]

Mix buttermilk, sour cream, beets, cucumbers, onions together. Blend vinegar and sugar, add to buttermilk mixture. Add eggs and shrimp just before serving.

82

Polish Meatballs
in Sour Cream

Sauté onion in ¼ cup of butter until it is soft. Combine meat, egg yolks, bread mixture, onion, dill, tarragon, salt and pepper to taste, in a large bowl. Beat egg whites, and fold into meat mixture. Form mixture into small balls and dust with flour. Brown the meatballs in a large fry pan in which you have put butter. Sauté mushrooms in the same skillet. Stir in sour cream, carefully, and simmer for 15 minutes, covered.

4 slices of bread soaked in a cup of milk
1 large onion chopped
½ cup butter
1 lb. ground beef [454 g]
1 lb. ground veal [454 g]
2 egg yolks
2 tbsp. chopped dill
1 tsp. tarragon
   salt and pepper
2 egg whites [beaten]
½ lb. mushrooms [227 g]
1½ cups sour cream

8. Pine Mushrooms and Erskine Lyons

Erskine Lyons warmed the brandy snifter for his father with a deftness that Jeeves might envy. Without Erskine, the party would have been less successful. Earlier he had spent an hour melting and gluing candle stubs together so that his parents would have longer, more elegant ones for their dinner table. He had also threaded the yaki-niku on skewers before broiling them — yaki-niku is kind of a Japanese pork kebab. Erskine is fifteen, wears blue jeans, long hair, and has that deadpan look (typical of his age) which may be interpreted as "There is nothing adults do or say that can surprise me anymore." Erskine's nonchalance and ease might be due in some way to his multi-cultural heritage. His father, Edward, born in Hamilton, Ontario, is half Scotch-Irish and half American-Jewish. Erskine's mother, Margaret, née Inouye, is British Columbian Japanese, born in the Fraser Valley. The gastronomic consequences are remarkable; Erskine, (named after his Scotch grandmother), can make Chelsea buns, (when he feels like it), and fries Japanese tempura in schmaltz. (Schmaltz is duck, chicken or goose fat Jewish people used to put in chopped liver, before they heard of cholesterol.)

That night, however, the dinner was what Margaret calls "B.C. Japanese." "Don't call it pure Japanese," she explained, "because I've never really been to Japan — only an hour stop-over at Tokyo airport." Margaret, her husband and Erskine live in Toronto, where Margaret is supervisor of Current Affairs Radio at the CBC, and Edward owns a survey company. Her family came to the Fraser Valley to farm from Japan at the end of the First World War. "My grandfather was never successful at making money, but he loved good food. On Japanese New Years, the house was cleaned from stem to stern; we ate sashimi, raw tuna, whole shrimps, rice cakes, and cooked octopus. The octopus hung from the ceiling; its tentacles looked three feet long, but then everything looks bigger when you're a child." Margaret says that octopus, cooked to a tenderness, not a toughness, tastes like a cross between abalone and lobster. The men would chop it in small pieces, and her mother would season it with mirin, (Japanese sherry), and a little vinegar.

Margaret's strongest memory is picking matsutake with her father in the hills above the Fraser Valley. Matsutake are pine mushrooms that are found in the compost under Douglas firs and red pines in British Columbia. Her father would sniff the air and announce that mushrooms were sprouting. "It was always the darkest, dankest, rainiest days when my father took us out looking for pine mushrooms; my mother was terrified that we'd get lost in the hills. But my father always knew where they were; he had his secret places. Sometimes after a day of picking, we would fill a one hundred pound sack. Pine mushrooms are cream-colored, and the cap can be as large as four inches, the stalk as thick as two inches. They look like huge toadstools and are the best mushrooms I've ever eaten. Father would sell what we didn't want to the Japanese greengrocer for a good price. All the Japanese in B.C. consider them a great delicacy. Even today you can buy them in Japanese shops in Vancouver, in season." Margaret's mother used to bottle them in brine and send the jars to Margaret in Toronto. "But they're best fresh, broiled, and eaten with a little soya sauce and sherry."

Margaret's family, like all the Japanese in British Columbia during the Second World War, were evacuated from their homes and interned in the Prairies. Margaret, still a teenager, took a job as a maid in Tuxedo, Winnipeg's poshest district, and at that time, a white Anglo-Saxon preserve. Although she came from a family that loved food, she was baffled when the lady of the house told her to cook a chicken. If you recall, in those days the butchers never bothered gutting a chicken. Neither did Margaret. She stayed on as a maid for two years, despite the chicken episode.

In 1944 she went to McMaster University to study economics, very much against her mother's wishes. Japanese girls were supposed to study flower arranging and sewing, not fluctuations of the stock market.

But Margaret's working experience as a teenager gave her a sense of independence that made her break with family tradition. She met Edward in 1949 in Hamilton, and they've been married twenty-five years.

The appearance, the arrangement of food play a greater role in Japanese cuisine than any other in the world. Ingredients are simple; a carrot, a slice of raw fish, a scallion, but each must satisfy the eye as well as the palate. The carrot might be trimmed so that it coils and curls, the scallion sprays out like a fountain, and the thin slices of raw fish, sashimi, are arranged like the petals of a flower on a fine porcelain plate. Long stewing and mingling of ingredients are not Japanese. The taste and texture of each vegetable and each piece of meat or fish are supposed to retain their distinctness. Portions are small, but each bowl or plate in classical Japanese cooking should be designed with the same care given to a traditional landscape brush and ink painting. Ginger root, bean curd (tofu), red and black lentils, dried seaweed, sesame seeds, shoyu or soy sauce, rice vinegar, fish, sliced very thin, and eaten raw, (sashimi), and rice, of course, are basics in Japanese cuisine.

Westerners who are fussy about good bread have something in common with Japanese people, who are fussy about their staple — rice. Margaret's family never buy the long grain converted rice; they prefer the round Japanese rice that can be bought at Japanese, and sometimes Chinese, delicatessens. The fresher the rice, the better it is, and the most desirable is always the most expensive.

Margaret Lyons, with her full-time job, house and family to look after, does not spend too much of her time carving radishes into lotus buds, or forming raw tuna slices into the shape of a heron in flight. Yet, every dish we ate that evening was arranged with a fastidiousness and appeal to the aesthetic sense that I have never seen equalled except for a meal I had years ago, at the Japanese Embassy in Ottawa. She spent one day shopping and one day cooking the dinner. As we sat in front of the fire in her living room, she brought out an exquisite platter containing sashimi, slightly flavored with a squeeze of lemon juice; kamaboko, a kind of fish paste or dumpling flavored with soy and ginger; barbecued eel and squid, dipped in vinegar and ground sesame seeds. Margaret cooked the squid herself. "Wash them, remove the ink sack, and boil them until they lose their translucence, just like shrimps."

At the table, we ate Erskine's yaki-niku, or pork kebab, that had sat overnight in a marinade of Japanese soy sauce, honey, sherry, garlic and boiling water. Margaret always keeps a jar of it in the refrigerator. Then came bowls of chawan-mushi, (literally "steamed in the bowl"): fresh vegetables, mushrooms, fish and chicken cooked in an egg custard. Each ingredient tasted distinct and separate. A salad of cold spinach flavored with vinegar and sprinkled with sesame seed accompanied the pièce de résistance, barbecued stuffed British Columbia salmon. Margaret says that no matter where Japanese live in Canada, they always look for B.C. products, especially fish. "British Columbian salmon is the best in the world," she announced, heedless of a Maritimer sitting in our midst.

Margaret Lyons' B.C. Japanese Salmon

Mix everything together, except the salmon, of course. Stuff the interior of the salmon with mixture, and sprinkle excess liquid over top of fish. Salt and pepper fish. Wrap fish in foil wrap completely, and bake for 30 to 45 minutes in a 350° F (175° C) oven. Make sure the fish does not overcook.

*(The dulse may be found in Newfoundland or in Japanese groceries.)

Serves 8

6 or 7 lb. salmon, fresh if possible [3.17 kg]
*1 cup dulse, or coarse dried sea weed
1 lb. mushrooms [454 g]
¾ to 1 lb. raw shrimp, chopped [454 g]
1 cup white wine or dry sherry
2 or 3 tbsp. shoyu [soy sauce] salt and pepper to taste

Japanese Fondue

One Pot Dish with Beef, Oysters and Mushrooms

4 oz. transparent noodles
  [harusame] [113 g]
2 lbs. Chinese cabbage,
  cut into chunks [907 g]
12 mushrooms
12 oysters or clams
12 to 16 canned gingko nuts
1 lb. beef in cubes [454 g]
6 slices boiled ham
80 oz. chicken stock
  [2.27 l]
3 tbsp. dry sherry
2 tbsp. shoyu
4 or 5 tsp. salt

Soak transparent noodles in cold water for 30 minutes. They should be soft when you drain and cut them into 4" lengths (10 cm). Arrange cabbage chunks, noodles, mushrooms, oysters, gingko nuts, ham and beef cubes and anything else you like attractively on a large platter.

Pour chicken stock, sherry, shoyu, salt in fondue pot, and heat until simmering. Everyone dips the foods from the platter into the simmering stock and cooks it as long or as little as he likes. The cooked vegetables may be dipped in tempura sauce, or 6 tbsp. of lemon juice mixed with 6 tbsp. of shoyu. Afterwards the broth will be even richer. Drink the soup after the meat and vegetables are eaten.

Japanese Spinach Salad

Margaret served this before the main course.

1 lb. fresh spinach [454 g]
1 cup water
2 tbsp. shoyu sauce
4 tbsp. sesame seeds
1 tbsp. sugar
1 tbsp. peanut oil
  juice ½ lemon

Wash, drain and cut spinach. Bring water to boil, add spinach and cook only until spinach has reduced in size, about 3 minutes. Drain thoroughly and cool. Toast sesame seeds in a fry pan over moderate heat; no oil is needed. Mix shoyu sauce, sugar, oil and lemon juice together. Mix into spinach. Portion spinach out into small saucers — you should have enough for about 4 or 5 people. Sprinkle toasted sesame seeds on top.

Clam or Oyster Soup

(The clam juice is a good substitute for kombu or dried kelp, which comes in hard black sheets. Pieces are cut off and used in soup stock. Kombu is available at Japanese groceries.)

Put oysters or clams in simmering chicken and clam juice stock. Add shoyu and sherry. Cook oysters only until they puff up. Cut lemon rind in small circles and use one to garnish each bowl of soup. Serve soup immediately.

12 to 16 oysters or clams [canned ones will not do]
1 tbsp. shoyu or soy sauce
2 tbsp. dry sherry
   lemon rind
2 cups canned clam juice
2 cups chicken soup

Fried Chicken

Slice chicken in thin slices. Mix sherry, shoyu, sugar and ginger, and bring to a boil. Use as marinade over raw chicken for ½ hour. Cut pepper in thin slices. Drain chicken and dust with cornstarch. Heat oil in fry pan, fry chicken, drain on absorbent paper. Fry pepper until just crisp.

Serve with tempura dipping sauce.

2 raw chicken breasts
3 tbsp. dry sherry
1 tbsp. shoyu
2 tsp. fresh ginger root, chopped
2 tbsp. sugar
1 red or green pepper
2 tbsp. cornstarch
5 tbsp. vegetable oil

Pork, Beef or Chicken Teriyaki with Soy and Honey Glaze

Charcoal grills and hibachis are perfect for this sort of cooking.

Margaret's Teriyaki Sauce

1 cup dry sherry
1 cup soy sauce
1 tbsp. honey
3 cloves chopped garlic
1 cup water
Boil together for
3 minutes.

2 lbs. of sirloin beef, or boneless chicken or pork, cut in cubes [907 g]

Take ½ cup of the teriyaki sauce, and mix in 1 tbsp. of cornstarch that has been softened with 1 tbsp. of water. To get a smooth texture and a clear glaze, cook it in a stainless steel pot. Set aside.

Pre-heat broiler to its highest point, or have hibachi grill ready. The meat may or may not be skewered. Dip meat into the glaze before cooking. Broil until the meat is lightly browned (Pork should be cooked longer than the chicken or beef.) Serve with the extra sauce.

Chawan-Mushi

Serves 4

Four 8 oz. custard cups or bowls [227 ml]
4 raw shrimp, or ¼ lb. of raw fish [sliced] [113 g]
½ lb. mushrooms [sliced] [227 g]

Beat eggs and add stock. Stir in salt and soy sauce. Divide beaten egg mixture into 4 bowls. Divide the vegetables and fish and meat in 4 portions and add to bowls. Cover bowls with foilwrap.

Use an Oriental steamer, or place bowls in a large pan of water and bake in a slow oven until custard is firm, about 15 minutes. Serve immediately.

½ **chicken breast [no bones, and sliced in strips]**
2 **cups chicken stock**
4 **eggs**
½ **lb. of a crisp vegetable, like broccoli or beans, cut up [227 g]**
½ **tsp. of shoyu, or soy sauce slices of fresh ginger root [optional] salt to taste**

Tempura

Tempura is one of the glories of Japanese cuisine. Practically any vegetable or firm fish may be used. Shrimp, broccoli, cauliflower, mushrooms, snow peas, asparagus and green beans are most commonly used.

Pre-heat oven to 250° F (120° C). To prepare batter, combine egg with ice water and baking soda in large mixing bowl. Sift in the flour and mix well. The batter should be thin and run off the spoon. If it is too thick, add several drops of water. Drop shrimp and vegetables in batter coating them well. Heat oil until it shows 375° F (190° C) on the thermometer. Drop shrimp and vegetables carefully into boiling oil, a little at a time. When the pieces are lightly browned, lay out in the pre-heated oven on paper towels and continue deep frying until all are cooked.

Each serving of tempura should be accompanied by the dipping sauce.

1 **lb. raw shrimp, or scallops [454 g]**
6 **large mushrooms**
1 **small cauliflower, cut into pieces a handful of snow peas or green beans**
4 **cups vegetable oil for deep frying**

Batter
1 **egg**
½ **cup ice cold water**
½ **tsp. baking soda**
1½ **cups flour**

Dipping Sauce

1 cup water
1 tbsp. dried fish flakes
   [bonito], optional
2 tbsp. shoyu
1 tsp. salt
2 tbsp. dry sherry or mirin
   chopped green onion for
   garnish

Boil water with fish flakes for 3 minutes. Strain. Add shoyu, sherry and salt. Boil. Cool. Just before serving, add green onion. Margaret's sauce, or 6 tbsp. of lemon juice with an equal amount of shoyu may be substituted.

9. Phyllo and Flowers

The first I heard of Greek cooking was from my girl friend Wendy Paulos (née Walker) who had just married and wanted to please her husband. He had come to Canada from Greece a decade before and missed the old country cooking. He longed for baked sheep's head. Wendy was only twenty and lived with her husband in Westmount, Montreal, where she, her parents and grandparents had been born. Westmount people eat lamb chops and kidney on occasion, but never the rest of the animal, whether in its immature or adult stage. But Wendy was eager and actually found what her husband pined for in one of the smaller, stranger butcher shops around St. Lawrence Street, in the east end of Montreal. She carried it home, wiped off the blood as best she could and put it in the oven. Every ten minutes or so she would open the oven door and stare at the head, which glared right back, though it was shrinking by the moment (except for the eye sockets). Wendy placed the baked head in front of her husband; he ate with relish, remarking only that it was inadequately seasoned. That was the first and last time Wendy cooked Greek food. Her husband was to blame; he never told her Greek cooking was much more than a shrivelled muttonhead with reproachful eyes that gave one troubled and guilty dreams. He never told her about roast leg of lamb, made succulent from a long bath in lemon juice and rosemary, or stuffed ripe tomatoes bursting with mint-flavored rice and pine nuts, or about a mysterious substance called phyllo, a pastry that looks and floats like white milk, yet remains crisp as the first fall ice on the Red River.

Phyllo pastry is used for many things in Greek cuisine. Sometimes it is stuffed with a spinach filling for pites, cut into little squares and served as an hors d'oeuvre, and sometimes it is stuffed with almonds and cinnamon and drenched in a sugar or honey syrup, flavored with lemon, for baklava, the most irresistible of all Greek sweets.

It is too bad Wendy never met Mrs. Helen Cholakis from Winnipeg. Mrs. Cholakis and her daughters-in-law are specialists in fine Greek

93

cooking, and make all the dishes I mentioned, with the exception of baked sheep's head.

The Cholakis family is well-known in Winnipeg. When their name is mentioned, two incongruous images come into the minds of local people — flowers and football. Paul Cholakis used to play for the Winnipeg Blue Bombers — an honor achieved by few Winnipeg boys, and the family owns the Broadway Florists, the largest flower business in town. Winnipeggers know about the flowers, and the new building near Eaton's, and the football, but few know about Mrs. Cholakis' cooking talents.

Mrs. Cholakis invited me for a Greek dinner, along with two of her sons, Paul and Chris, and their wives. The house was full of fresh flowers, spider mums and irises, and we drank ouzo and ate Cathy's tarama salata. Cathy is Paul's wife, and tarama salata is a dip or spread made out of fish roe, oil and lemon juice, day-old bread, and a boiled mashed potato. (The ingredients sound pedestrian, but their combination produces remarkable results.) While we ate, Helen Cholakis told me about the early years in Winnipeg.

In 1920, Ernest Cholakis, Mrs. Cholakis' husband, was on his way to Seattle from New York to open a flower business, but he took ill on the train and had to get off at Winnipeg. When he got out of the St. Boniface Hospital it was January. He looked at the snow, felt the bracing 40° below wind, and realized that Winnipeggers, very clearly, needed flowers more than did the people in Seattle where the rosebuds were already set on the branches. He started up a successful flower business but had to go as far as Birmingham, Alabama, to find a nice Greek girl for a bride. (Mrs. Cholakis still speaks with a soft southern accent despite her years in Winnipeg.)

During the 1930's the Cholakises settled in Norwood, a section of Winnipeg where there were no Greeks living at all. (At that time there were only about twenty-five Greek families living in the city.) Mrs. Cholakis wanted her five boys to look decent, and made them wear white shirts and ties everyday to school. The Scotch-Irish kids living in Norwood saw no reason for the Cholakis boys to wear Sunday clothes everyday and blackened their eyes and bloodied their noses, everyday. (Paul says the code word before the attack was "greasy Greeks".) Whatever the Cholakis boys felt at the time, they don't deny it was excellent training for the Blue Bombers.

When we sat down to dinner, Mrs. Cholakis served grape leaves stuffed with rice and ground meat, smothered with avgolemono or egg-lemon sauce, as the first course. She remembers when she used to pick wild grape leaves north of Winnipeg, in order to prepare the dish, but now she buys them at a Chinese or Italian grocery, and even at Eaton's. Mrs. Cholakis reminisced, "Then everything was different. I used to spend from 3:30 to 5:30, seven days a week, preparing dinner for my family." Mrs. Cholakis' husband died a few years ago, and she sounded as if she missed those years, cooking for him and the five boys, and their football friends.

A plate of pites was passed around, made by Mrs. Fotoula Vlassie, who by general acclaim is "number one phyllo-maker in Winnipeg." Mrs. Vlassie stretches her phyllo dough over a pillow on the kitchen table, so that it reaches the right degree of thinness without tearing. "It's easy," she said "one , two, three and it's done." (I tried it, "one, two and three" and the result was thick enough to side a barn.)

Mrs. Vlassie is a real old-timer. When she first came to Winnipeg fifty-five years ago from Corinth, Greece, she wanted to throw herself off the Osborne Street Bridge because of the cold, but changed her mind, married George Vlassie, and they opened one of Winnipeg's oldest and best tearooms, the Chocolate Shop. Her eldest son, Nick, was killed in the Second World War. "Mrs. Vlassie taught us everything about cooking," Mrs. Cholakis says.

After giving Mrs. Vlassie her due, Helen Cholakis brought out her roast leg of lamb that had been sitting in a marinade of lemon and rosemary for twenty-four hours before she baked it. Then we had the pastries and fruit.

Greeks love sweet pastries made from phyllo dough and nuts, drenched with honey and sugar syrups. We ate baklava, the best I've ever tasted, made by Mrs. Vlassie, who uses butter, (never shortening), and boils a whole orange and lemon in her sugar syrup to add interest to the sweetness. Lillian, Chris' wife, made kourambiethes, which she described as "Greek shortbread" made from ground nuts and lots of butter. Mrs. Cholakis made copenhie, another pastry with phyllo dough, like baklava, but with eggs mixed in with the nuts. Lillian is carrying on the Greek tradition of cooking — she made five thousand stuffed tomatoes for Winnipeg's Folkerama Festival in the summer of '74.

While we ate the pastries, Mrs. Cholakis brought out sweet, strong (if the Greeks will forgive me) Turkish Coffee, which is also traditionally Greek. The boys urged Mrs. Vlassie to "read the cups." She turned down each of our demitasses and looked at the pattern the dregs made of the fine powdered coffee. When she saw something she didn't like, she kept quiet, and told us only of the good things, trips, and money coming from somewhere. However, I was warned to beware of a stout woman with something like a crown on her head who has it in for me. I've been looking over my shoulder ever since.

Tarama Salata

4 slices day old bread [use two more if you don't use the potato]
1 cup cold water
4 oz. fish roe [114 g]
juice of 2 or 3 lemons
½ a grated lemon
1 mashed potato [optional]
½ cup salad or olive oil, or better still, a mixture of the two

This makes a good spread or dip to go with drinks. If you see the word Tarama on the jar, you'll know you've got what the Greeks buy, but any fish roe will do: carp, cod or even salmon caviar. Carp and cod are of course much cheaper than salmon roe, as well as being more authentic. A blender is best for this dish. If you haven't a blender, a rotary electric beater will do.

Soak bread in water and squeeze dry. Combine it with the fish roe in blender. Blend until smooth and add lemon juice, grated onion,

96

mashed potato and finally the oil in a slow stream. The amount of lemon juice and oil can be varied to your taste. Served with toast or crackers as an hors d'oeuvre.

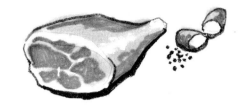

Helen Cholakis' Roast Lamb

Trim excess fat from meat. Wipe lamb with damp cloth and place skin side up on rack in roasting pan. Make small slits in skin and insert slivers of garlic. Salt and pepper meat generously. Sprinkle oregano over meat. Melt butter, pour lemon juice and melted butter over meat. Add onions and ½ cup of water to pan, lower temperature to 350° F (175° C) and roast about 2 hours, basting occasionally. (Mrs. Cholakis roasts quartered potatoes in the gravy along with the meat. Add them ½ hour after meat has been cooking.)

Preheat oven to 500° F [260° C]

5 lb. leg of lamb [2.27 kg]
2 cloves garlic
 salt and pepper
1 tsp. oregano
⅓ cup butter
 juice of large lemon [or two small lemons]
2 onions chopped
3 or 4 sprigs parsley

Note: This is full of flavor. If you use a frozen leg of lamb, the lemon removes any strong taste of mutton.

Baklava   One of the best sweets in the world

Making phyllo pastry is an art. If you know someone like Mrs. Vlassie, ask her to show you how to do it. Following the instructions from a recipe is difficult. The pulling and stretching of

97

the dough are of critical importance. In the large cities it is possible to buy frozen phyllo dough at Greek and Lebanese groceries or bakeries.

2 lbs. chopped nuts [almonds, pecans or walnuts] [907 g]
¼ tsp. ground cloves
½ cup sugar
1 lb. clarified butter [454 g]
1 lb. phyllo pastry [454 g]

Syrup
4 cups sugar
2 cups water
juice of 1 lemon
1 stick of cinnamon
4 tbsp. honey

Mix together. Boil 10 minutes. Cool slightly, pour over warm baklava.

Combine nuts, cloves and sugar, mix well. Grease a 17½" x 12½" x 2" pan (44.5 cm x 31.75 cm x 5.1 cm) with a little melted butter. Place 8 sheets of phyllo in pan, brushing each with melted butter. Sprinkle with layer of nut mixture, cover with 3 phyllo sheets, brushing each with butter and sprinkling top sheet with nut mixture. Continue the 3 phyllo procedure until all the nuts have been used. Top with 6 phyllo sheets, brushing each with melted butter. With a sharp knife cut into small squares. Bake in pre-heated oven for 1½ hours at 300° F (150° C). Remove from oven and pour cool syrup over baklava.

The baklava is eaten cold, with coffee.

Spanakopittes (Spinach Pie)

or Pites, as they say in Winnipeg

1 lb. phyllo pastry [454 g]
2 lbs. fresh or frozen spinach chopped [907 g]
3 tbsp. olive oil
5 eggs, beaten
1 cup chopped onions [scallions or plain cooking onions]
½ cup butter

A wonderful hors d'oeuvre or luncheon dish.

Cook spinach in olive oil until wilted. Drain. Brown cooking onions in half a cup of butter. Mix onions, eggs, cheese, dill and parsley together. Add spinach and season with salt and pepper. Butter a 17½" x 12½" x 2" pan (44.5 cm x 31.75 cm x 5.1 cm) and place 8 to 10 phyllo pastry sheets in the pan, brushing the melted sweet butter in between the sheets. Spread spinach mixture evenly on top. Cover with 8 to 10 pastry sheets, brushing each with butter. With a sharp knife cut through the top to mark into one or two inch squares. Bake in a pre-heated oven for one hour or until golden brown and very puffy. Cut into squares and serve hot or cold.

½ **lb. feta cheese, crumbled, or dry cottage cheese [227 g]**
½ **cup chopped fresh dill and parsley**
1 **cup melted sweet butter salt and pepper to taste Pre-heat oven to 350° F [175° C]**

Kourambiethes   Greek Shortbread

Makes about 4 dozen ("You must use clarified butter," Mrs. Cholakis told me.)

Clarify butter, refrigerate until the consistency is soft. Whip with electric beater until light and fluffy, about 10 minutes. Add sugar, beat until smooth (about 5 minutes), add egg yolk, and whisky. Beat well. Add sifted flour, a little at a time beating constantly, until a soft dough is formed that can be handled easily. Work together slightly with hands. Pinch off 2 tablespoons of dough at a time, shaping it into an oval or crescent. Place cookies 1 inch apart on an ungreased baking pan and bake at 325° F (165° C) for 15 minutes, and 275° F (135° C) for 30 minutes, or until they are lightly browned. Handling them carefully, sprinkle immediately with icing sugar. This should be done while they are still warm. They may be frozen, but sprinkle with extra sugar after thawing.

1 **lb. butter, clarified [454 g]**
4 **tbsp. icing sugar**
1 **egg yolk**
1 **jigger whisky**
3½ **to 3¾ cups all-purpose flour, sifted about 3 cups icing sugar for dusting cookies [dust heavily]**

Dolmathes (Stuffed Grape Leaves)

9 oz. jar of grape leaves, or about 40 fresh grape leaves   [250 ml]
1 large grated onion
3 tbsp. butter
1½ lbs. ground beef [680 g]
2 tsp. of chopped parsley and mint [or one or the other]
¼ cup cooked rice
salt and pepper to taste
2 cups chicken or beef broth

Drain brine from grape leaves.   Rinse them thoroughly.   Parboil in water for 5 minutes.

To prepare filling for leaves, sauté onion in butter.   Place meat in mixing bowl, add onions, parsley, mint, rice, salt and pepper.   Mix together well.   When filling leaves, keep the shiny side of the leaf outside.   Put 1 large tsp. of filling in the center of leaf and fold the sides up over it like an envelope.   Then roll into a cylindrical shape.   Place a few grape leaves in bottom of a saucepan and then carefully arrange the dolmathes in layers.   Add broth and simmer for 1 hour until done.   Prepare egg-lemon sauce and pour over dolmathes.

Avgolemono Saltsa (Egg-Lemon Sauce)

3 eggs well beaten
juice of 2 lemons
about 1 cup of liquid from the dolmathes

Use double boiler or a pot over low heat if you are deft.   Beat eggs until light and fluffy.   Add lemon juice slowly.   Gradually add about a cup of hot but not boiling liquid from the dolmathes, beating constantly.   Pour sauce over drained dolmathes.   Shake saucepan to spread evenly.

10. Christmas in August

I knew three things about Icelanders when I was a young girl in Winnipeg.

1. Winnipeg has more Icelanders than Reykjavik, the capital of Iceland.
2. Girls with pale blond hair and lean flanks and names like Einarson and Sigurdson were the only ones who looked good in the pleated tunic, bloomers and lisle stockings we had to wear in Winnipeg's public schools.
3. The best cake in Manitoba was an Icelandic specialty, vinaterta, seven layers of butter rich pastry, stuffed with prunes and cardamom and covered with almond icing.

Professor Haralder Bessason, who specializes in Icelandic studies at the University of Winnipeg, was born in Iceland, unlike most people of Icelandic descent who live in Winnipeg. He says that vinaterta in Iceland has only three layers. A mutation took place in Manitoba, and four more butter pastry layers were added to the original species — a bigger cake for a bigger country. In Iceland they stuff their cake with strawberries or rhubarb, an unknown custom here. According to the history of Manitoba's Icelanders, prunes and only prunes have been the documented filling between the leaves of Manitoba's vinaterta.

Icelanders settled in Manitoba between 1875 and 1910 because volcanoes erupted and laid waste their country. The first group of Icelanders had a terrible beginning — one third of the community died of smallpox. Later groups were decimated by scurvy. Yet in 1877 an astonishing event occurred, unique in Canada's history. A separate state was set up in the Keewatin district; the Republic of New Iceland was proclaimed, a constitution drafted, a ruling council organized, and Gimli, Manitoba, was made the capital. New Iceland's autonomy lasted for one whole year, until someone back in Ottawa finally took a look at the consequences of having a separate nation in the heart of Canada and gave the republic of New Iceland back to Manitoba.

It's been a long time since that burst of separatist glory; the Icelanders now are one of the most assimilated groups in Canada. They started off as fishermen and farmers, but most have left the fields and lakes to become professional and business people, not to mention politicians.

Icelandic traditions are mainly remembered at Christmas time. Doris Johnson, wife of Dr. George, (pater familias to all Manitoba Icelanders, former provincial cabinet minister, and medical man), always sets a table of Icelandic specialties after the Lutheran carol service. She serves the traditional hot chocolate, rullu pylsa, (pickled spiced lamb), lifrar-pylsa, (liver sausage), mysuostur, a special cheese spread, homemade brown bread, and all kinds of Icelandic cookies and cakes.

It was a hot August day, when Doris prepared an Icelandic Christmas dinner for twenty guests, including myself. Doris was helped by her mother, Mrs. Gudrun Blondal, who was on the verge of celebrating her 80th birthday, and her mother-in-law, Mrs. Laufy Johnson; neither lady sat down all evening.

These recipes are all from Doris Johnson, Mrs. Blondal, and Mrs. Laufy Johnson.

Rullu Pylsa
Spiced lamb. Excellent for Christmas holidays

Chop one large or two small onions very fine. Mix with spices. Arrange meat so fat and lean alternate, or remove some fat. Sprinkle with onions and spices. Roll up as a jelly roll. Skewer to hold roll in shape. Sew up well with firm string. Wrap roll all around with a very strong string and tie up well. Rub on outside with a bit of salt and saltpeter. Wrap loosely in wax paper. Store in refrigerator 3 or 4 days, turning over each day. Boil in slightly salted water for 2 hours, and press between two plates until cold. Do not use heavy weights. Slice very thin and serve on bread.

- 4½ lbs. lamb flanks, with bones removed [2 kg]
- 2 tbsp. salt
- 1 tbsp. brown sugar
- ½ tsp. saltpeter
- ½ tsp. cloves
- 1 tsp. allspice
- ½ tsp. pepper
  onions

Lifrar-Pylsa
Liver sausage

This is not difficult to make. The rolled oats and whole wheat flour will appeal to those who worry about getting enough roughage in their system.

Put mixture in a casserole, cover, and put casserole in a pan of hot water. Bake 2½ hours at 325° F (165° C). Remove cover and bake 15 minutes longer.

- ¾ lb. liver, put through grinder [340 g]
- ½ lb. kidney suet [227 g]
- 1 cup rolled oats
- ¾ cup whole wheat flour
- 1 cup milk
- 1 cup water
- 2 tsp. salt
- 1 tsp. brown sugar

Mysuostur

This is a sweet cheese spread that Icelanders love with brown bread.

½ lb. whey cheese [227 g]
½ cup Carnation milk
½ cup brown sugar
¼ cup margarine or butter
1 tbsp. butter

Break whey cheese up into small pieces and put into top of a double boiler. Add milk (undiluted), brown sugar, and heat at low temperature until soft. Add margarine or butter and beat well. Put mixture into a sealer or jar, and when cool, store in refrigerator.

Pönnukökur   Icelandic crêpes

3 eggs well-beaten
½ cup sugar
2 tbsp. butter
½ tsp. cinnamon
1 tsp. vanilla
½ cup sour cream
½ tsp. soda
1½ cup flour
1 tsp. baking powder
¼ tsp. salt
2 cups [or a little more] sweet milk

Beat eggs. Add well-creamed sugar and butter. Add cinnamon and vanilla. Dissolve soda in a little boiling water and mix with sour cream. Add flour and baking powder and salt sifted together. Beat well and gradually stir in sweet milk. To bake, use a fairly heavy griddle pan. Rub butter or shortening on pan. Lift pan off hot element while you pour in 1/5th cup batter. Tip griddle around until entire bottom is covered. Set griddle back on hot element as quickly as possible. Brown lightly on both sides.

After they leave the griddle, Doris lets them cool and then spreads whipped cream on them. She rolls them up, sprinkles them with icing sugar, and serves them as a dessert.

Astar Bollur

These little balls are Mrs. Blondal's specialty.

Cream butter, add sugar, eggs, milk and flavoring. Gradually add the sifted dry ingredients. Mix well. Add raisins. Drop by teaspoon into hot oil 375° F (190° C); they will turn over of their own accord when baked on bottom. Cook until brown, 2 to 3 minutes. Drain on absorbent paper. The balls may be rolled in icing sugar.

A good method for dripping batter into oil is to use one spoon to drop batter and another spoon, dipped in the hot oil, to shape the balls into a rounder, more even shape.

butter, size of walnut
¾ cup sugar
2 well-beaten eggs
1¼ cup milk
1 tsp. vanilla
½ tsp. nutmeg
2 cups flour [or a bit more]
2 tsp. baking powder
½ cup raisins
2 cups vegetable oil or lard

Vinaterta

The crowning achievement of Icelandic cookery.

Should be made 24 to 48 hours before serving.

Mix batter in order given. Take care not to use too much flour. Divide dough into six or seven balls. Chill. Roll out balls one at a time. They should have a rich cookie dough texture. Bake each on bottom of a circular 8″ (20 cm) pan at 375° F (190° C) for 10-15 minutes.

Batter

1½ cup white sugar
1 cup butter
3 large eggs
3 tsp. baking powder
½ cup milk
1 tsp. vanilla
1 tsp. almond flavoring
3¾ cup flour
½ tsp. salt

Filling

1½ lbs. prunes [680 g]
2½ cup white sugar
1 tsp. cardamom

Cover the prunes with water and boil until prunes are soft and most of the water absorbed. Cool. Run stoned prunes through grinder, add the sugar and cardamom seed ground fine. Heat thoroughly, stirring constantly. Allow to cool.

Spread filling between cake layers placed on top of one another. If desired, ice the top of the cake with butter icing, flavored with almond extract. Cardamom powder may be used instead of cardamom seeds, shelled and ground, but the seed has more flavor.

Gravlax

More Swedish than Icelandic, this is one of the finest dishes in the world.

1 whole salmon, about 6 or 7 lbs. [3.17 kg] [ask your fish dealer to saw through the frozen fish lengthwise to make two slabs]
2 bunches of fresh dill [or dill seed if fresh is unavailable]
½ cup coarse salt [or pickling salt]
½ cup sugar
4 tbsp. peppercorns [crushed], preferably white

Defrost fish. Place half of fish, skin side down, in a glass, enamel or stainless steel baking dish. Chop dill and place it over fish. Combine sugar, salt and crushed peppercorns in a separate bowl. Spread this mixture over dill. Top with other half of fish, skin side up. Cover with aluminum foil, and on it set a heavy platter or a board larger than the salmon. Pile the platter or board with several cans of food as weights. Refrigerate 3 days.

Turn fish every 12 hours, basting it with liquid marinade that accumulates, separating the halves a little to baste the salmon inside. Replace the platters and weights each time.

When the gravlax is fully marinated, remove fish from liquid; scrape away dill and seasonings and pat dry. Place separated halves, skin side down, on a carving board and slice the salmon thinly on the diagonal, removing the skin as best you can.

Serves 10 to 12 people.

Mustard Sauce

In a small bowl mix the mustards, sugar, and vinegar to a paste. Add whole egg, beating hard. With a wire whisk, slowly beat in the oil until it forms a mayonnaise. Stir in fresh dill.

You may keep this in your refrigerator for several days; just beat it up again before serving.

The same sauce can be made in a blender: Add egg, mustards, sugar, salt and vinegar to blender. Then pour in oil while blender is working.

8 tbsp. French mustard [Dijon type]
2 tsp. powdered English mustard
6 tsp. sugar
4 tbsp. white vinegar
1 whole egg
2/3 cup vegetable oil
as much fresh chopped dill as you like

11. Manitoba's Mennonites

Eric Friesen, host announcer for the CBC in Winnipeg, looked at my recipe for turkey stuffing and shook his head doubtfully. "It won't taste as good as bubbat." "Bubbat? What's bubbat?" I said. Eric became enthusiastic. "My mother always stuffs the Christmas turkey with bubbat. We eat plumi moos and fleisch perishky with it; and some homemade farmer's sausage that I get at a little place just outside Morden."

Eric comes from a Manitoba Mennonite family and loves to talk about food. Morden, Winkler, Altona and Steinbach are Mennonite towns in Manitoba, and surnames like Friesen, Klassen, Penner and Reimer are as familiar to Manitobans as wheat and wide streets.

The Mennonites are a religious group, primarily interested in farming, who came to Manitoba over one hundred years ago from south Russia. Unlike the Doukhobors or Hutterites, the Mennonites never lived in farming communes, and their hold on their children and grandchildren has always been more relaxed. Manitoba Mennonites have entered into every aspect of Canadian life: business, medicine, the universities, and politics. Even the army, although the taking up of arms is against the Mennonite religion. Most Mennonite names can be traced to Dutch and Flemish origins, if you go as far back as 1400. During the late seventeenth century, however, they began to speak a Low German dialect instead of Dutch, because they were living in Danzig, then part of Prussia. Religious persecution forced them to leave Danzig and settle in southern Russia, where they lived for almost one hundred and fifty years before they came to Manitoba in 1874. Their cooking style reflects their wanderings, a taste of Dutch, more than a cup of German, all stirred with a Slavic spoon. One hundred years in Manitoba have added banana chiffon cakes and low-cal cheesecake to local Mennonite recipe books.

Manitoba's Mennonites have little in common with the Mennonites from Kitchener-Waterloo county in Ontario. The old Amish, as the earliest and strictest group is called, came from Switzerland and the Rhineland, and stopped off in Pennsylvania before settling in Ontario in 1800.

There is nothing Russian in Ontario Mennonite cuisine, like paska (an egg-rich Easter bread) or warenicki, (known in the Canadian vernacular as perogies), yet paska and warenicki are very much a part of the Manitoba Mennonite repertoire.

The Ontario Mennonites specialize in dishes of a purer German or Swiss German origin, shoo fly pies with a wet molasses bottom, deep-fried raised dough fritters, pork hocks and sauerbrauten.

Steinbach "the automobile city of Manitoba" was the center of the Manitoba Mennonite Centennial celebrations in 1974. It's one of the most successful towns in the province. The surrounding farmland is called Winnipeg's milkshed, and the prosperous automobile and farm machinery dealers, whose salesrooms line the main street, make sure there are no parking meters to discourage the shoppers. The people in the area built a permanent Mennonite Museum, filled it with pioneer artifacts and brought an original Mennonite house and barn all the way from Winkler, and set them down not far from the windblown grist mill.

The museum grounds had homecooked Mennonite food for sale. I headed for a shed behind the museum and found Mrs. Peter Rosenfeld, author of "The Mennonite Treasury of Recipes" and chief cook for the centennial celebrations, standing over two huge vats of borsch. "One for summer, one for winter," she explained. The summer borsch was green, with the flavor of dill and another herb or vegetable I couldn't place. "That's sorrel," said Mrs. Rosenfeld, "We all grow sorrel in our vegetable gardens, because it's the best leaf to put in summer borsch. Our grandparents brought the seeds over from Russia one hundred years ago, and we've been growing it ever since." Later on I saw the sorrel growing in the farmhouse garden. Sorrel has a thinner, paler leaf than spinach, and is more acid in flavor; the young leaves are sometimes called sour grass.

The winter borsch was red, rich with cabbage, ham and beef bones and tomatoes, a real Slavic soup. Another lady brought me some of her farmer's sausage, the kind that Eric Friesen mentioned, juicy and tasty, totally unlike the mass-produced, artificially preserved sausage you buy at the supermarket delicatessen. "The pig was killed just five days ago," she told me.

The Mennonites used to make pig-butchering into a kind of bee. Several families got together before dawn so the day would be long enough to make sausages, liverwurst, lard and headcheese after the pigs were killed. In the evening they would all sit down to a supper of "repschpa," (spareribs cooked in the fresh lard until the bone could be loosened by giving it a twist), fried potatoes and cracklings, homemade mustard, liverwurst, and plumi moos, a simmered mixture of dried apricots, prunes, raisins and apples, spiced with cloves and thickened with milk and flour. An anonymous writer in Mrs. Rosenfeld's cookbook asks, "Looking back, was there anything more exciting than butchering, except perhaps Christmas?"

My companion for the rest of the day was Mrs. Bill Enns, secretary of the ladies auxiliary of the Mennonite Museum. Mrs. Enns makes her own noodles, and sells them to "the few ladies in Steinbach who don't make their own." She took me around the food stands on the museum grounds. First we ate roll kuchen with watermelon; roll kuchen is an unsweetened pastry that has been deep-fried; it is traditionally eaten with watermelon or borsch. The roll kuchen reveals the Dutch-German heritage, while the watermelon and borsch can only be south Russian. Watermelon preserves occupy a fair space in the jams and jellies section of Manitoba Mennonite cookbooks.

We went over to the waffles shed; waffles were cooked to the ultimate in crispness on old-fashioned iron barrels. We ate cabbage rolls, brown bread, made from the flour of the grist mill, and gooseberry platz, an open tart with a soft rich dough and gooseberries on top. Gooseberries were once held in contempt. In earlier days, Mennonites called the poorer of their neighbors, with small farm holdings, "gooseberry farmers."

Bubbat

Eric's favorite stuffing for chicken or turkey. You might call it a Mennonite version of Yorkshire pudding.

Mix dry ingredients, add beaten egg, shortening and milk. Mix well and add raisins. Bake in 350° F (175° C) oven for 20 minutes in same pan with chicken, or stuff chicken with mixture and bake it as long as you roast the chicken.

1 cup flour
1½ tsp. baking powder
2 tbsp. butter or shortening melted
1 egg
⅓ cup milk
1 cup raisins

Piroshki

Mrs. Enns uses a yeast dough for her meat piroshki. However, a pie dough will do.

Dissolve yeast and sugar in warm water in a large bowl. Scald milk and cool. Add to yeast. Add remaining ingredients to make a soft dough. Let rise for about one hour or until doubled in bulk.

Combine all ingredients. Roll out dough ¼" thick (6 mm). Place dabs of meat mixture on dough far enough from the edge so dough can be folded over filling, just far enough to cover it. Then cut ½ circles with a round cutter. The straight side is the fold part of the dough. Set them on baking sheet with fold side down and pinched edges up. Bake in 350° F (175° C) for 30 minutes.

Yeast Dough

½ cup warm water
1 package dry yeast
1 cup scalded milk
1 tbsp. sugar
½ cup shortening
1½ tsp. salt
3 cups of flour

Filling

1 cup coarsely grated potatoes
½ cup carrots
1 small onion, grated
½ lb. raw ground round steak, minced cooked beef, pork or chicken [Mrs. Enns adds a little sage with the chicken.] [227 g]
2 tbsp. chopped parsley
1 tsp. salt
pepper

Plumi Moos

80 oz. water [2.28 l]
1 cup prunes
1 cup dried peaches or apricots
1 cup dried apples
1 cup raisins
about 1 tbsp. cinnamon
½ tsp. salt
½ cup sugar
½ cup cornstarch

Fruit soup. This may be served warm or cold with sausages, cold meats, or by itself. It makes a good dessert.

Cook fruit in water until tender. Prepare a paste with cornstarch, sugar and salt, and ½ cup of water. Slowly add paste to simmering fruit, add cinnamon, cook until slightly thickened. Delicious with whipped cream.

Fruit Piroshki

Mr. Enns takes these fishing with him because he believes they bring him good luck.

1 cup sugar
1 cup sour cream
½ cup butter
3 eggs
1 tsp. soda
1 tsp. baking powder
the juice from ½ a lemon and rind
enough flour to make soft dough, about 4 cups.

Cream butter and sugar. Add eggs and beat well. Sift dry ingredients and add alternately with sour cream. Roll out and cut with large round cookie cutter, or into 3" squares (7.5 cm). On each round or square, place some cut apple or whatever fruit is available: cherries, apricots, rhubarb or blueberries. Add a tbsp. of sugar and lemon juice and rind, and seal dough so that the fruit juice will not run out. Bake at 425° F (220° C), till brown.

Summer or Sorrel Soup

If you have no sorrel, other options are spinach, or beet tops.

Pour vegetables in soup stock. Simmer until potatoes are cooked. Add sour cream and cream just before serving.

80 oz. soup stock made by boiling ham bone in water for 1 hr. [2.28 l]
3 cups finely chopped sorrel leaves, or beet greens, or spinach leaves.
½ cup chopped fresh dill
1 cup chopped green onions
5 medium potatoes, diced salt and pepper to taste
½ cup sweet cream
1 cup thick sour cream [optional]

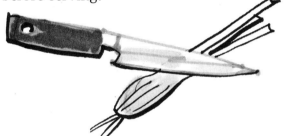

Preserved Watermelon Rind Slices

a great favorite with Manitoba Mennonites

Remove pink meat and hard green skin from watermelon rind. Cut rind in slices. Take about 4 quarts of the rind (4.5 l) and combine with cold water and salt. Let stand overnight. Drain and rinse well next day. Combine boiling water with rest of ingredients. Bring to a boil and add rind. Boil until rind is transparent, about 45 minutes. Seal in jam jars.

1 watermelon
120 oz. cold water [3.4 l]
½ cup salt
1½ cups boiling water
3 cups cider vinegar
6 cups sugar
1 tbsp. red food coloring [optional]
1 tbsp. mixed pickling spices peel of large lemon, cut in slices

Watermelon Pickle
using the pink meat

2 cups water
1 cup vinegar
6 tbsp. sugar
1 cut watermelon
1 tbsp. salt
¾ tbsp. alum
  few sprigs of dill

Cook syrup 5 minutes. Add watermelon and bring to a boil.

Pack watermelon pickle into hot sterilized jars to within ½ inch (1.25 cm) of the jar tops. Seal firmly with caps and rings.

Place jars in boiling water bath for 5 minutes. Water should be 1 inch (2.54 cm) above jars. Store.

Dutch Red Eggs   for picnics and snacks

3 cups water
2 cups vinegar
1 tsp. whole cloves
½ tsp. celery seed
1 tsp. peppercorns
1½ tsp. salt
  Beet juice from pickled
  beets, or from a can of
  beets, to give eggs a
  red color.
12 hard-boiled eggs

Bring spices and liquid to a boil. Simmer for 15 minutes. Put cooled hard-boiled eggs in glass jars and pour liquid into jars. Refrigerate for 3 days.

Roast Goose with Sauerkraut and Caraway Seeds

Cook onions in goose fat until golden brown. Drain sauerkraut and rinse in cold water. Add sauerkraut to onions. Add bread crumbs, chopped apples, caraway seeds, pepper and salt to taste.

Stuff goose. Place in a shallow roasting pan, preferably over a rack, so the fat will drip away from the bird. Cook at 350° F (175° C) for 3 hours. Prick the skin to let the fat run out. Drain off fat periodically. Just before serving remove all fat from the gravy. Roast goose can be served with plumi moos.

8 lb. to 10 lb. goose [3.60 kg to 4.5 kg]

Sauerkraut Stuffing

2 large onions chopped
2 tbsp. goose fat
2 lbs. sauerkraut [907 g]
2 cups bread crumbs [a little more if you think it necessary to fill the cavity]
2 tsp. caraway seed
2 unpeeled chopped apples
salt and pepper to taste

Carrot Nut Raisin Spice Cake

Set oven at 350° F (175° C). Grease an angel tube pan. Beat oil and sugar with mixer until very well blended. Sift soda, baking powder, flour, salt, and spices together and add about one-third to sugar mixture. Blend again.

Add remaining dry ingredients alternately with the whole eggs. Mix well after each addition. Your batter will be quite thick, but the carrots will provide the moisture for the cake. Add carrots, nuts and raisins. Pour batter in tube pan and bake for 1 hour. When done, invert cake on rack and let cool. Freezes well.

1¼ cups salad oil [not olive oil]
2 cups granulated sugar
2 cups all-purpose flour
2 tsp. baking powder
1 tsp. soda
1 tsp. salt
1 tsp. ginger
4 tsp. cinnamon
1 tsp. each mace and nutmeg
4 eggs
3 cups grated raw carrots
1 cup chopped walnuts
1 cup raisins

Sour Cream Icing

2 cups sour cream
   juice of 2 oranges
1⅔ cups icing sugar
   juice of 1 lemon

Since sour cream is one of the most important ingredients in the Mennonite cooking of Waterloo County, this recipe for sour cream icing has a certain logic.

Boil ingredients to 225° F (108° C). Cool and spread on cake. (You might have some left for a filling.)

Edna Staebler's Funnel Cake

3 tbsp. sour cream
2 eggs well-beaten
   not quite 2 cups milk
1 tsp. baking powder
3 cups flour
½ tsp. soda
½ tsp. salt

Measure the sour cream into a cup and fill the cup with milk, then stir the milk into the beaten eggs. Sift the dry ingredients into the egg and milk mixture and beat until smooth. If the batter isn't runny, you will have to add more milk. Heat deep fat until it browns a cube of bread or reaches 375° F (190° C). Pour batter into a small pitcher so it will be easier to handle.

Now comes the fun. Put your finger over the spout of a funnel and pour about 3 tbsp. of the batter into the funnel. Remove your finger and let the batter run into the hot fat, swirling the funnel around so the batter forms a lacy pattern or concentric circles about 3" to 6" (7.6 cm to 15.25 cm) in diameter. It's best to make swirls moving out from the center. The frying becomes quite an art as you learn to make quick twirls and turns of the funnel, covering and uncovering the opening. It's not as hard as it sounds.

Fry the cakes until they are golden brown; then drain them on paper towels and serve hot, sprinkled with powdered sugar.

12. Buckwheat and Honey

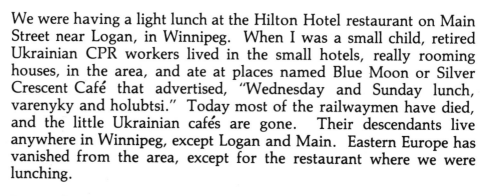

Just before we tucked into our varenyky-pyrohy (yellow cheese and potato), or as they say in the western Canadian vernacular, perogies, Bonnie Gerus sniffed the bowl of sour cream suspiciously. "I think it's commercial," she whispered.

We were having a light lunch at the Hilton Hotel restaurant on Main Street near Logan, in Winnipeg. When I was a small child, retired Ukrainian CPR workers lived in the small hotels, really rooming houses, in the area, and ate at places named Blue Moon or Silver Crescent Café that advertised, "Wednesday and Sunday lunch, varenyky and holubtsi." Today most of the railwaymen have died, and the little Ukrainian cafés are gone. Their descendants live anywhere in Winnipeg, except Logan and Main. Eastern Europe has vanished from the area, except for the restaurant where we were lunching.

Bonnie finally asked the waitress in Ukrainian if the sour cream was commercially made. The waitress, embarrassed, answered, in Ukrainian and English, "It is, it is, but taste the varenyky; the lady who makes them knows what she's doing. I bet you've never tasted deep-fried varenyky." Bonnie didn't touch the sour cream, but she admitted that the deep-fried varenyky, though a novelty, were excellent.

There is a continuing controversy about the difference between varenyky, pyrohy and perogies. You can safely describe all of them as curvacious ravioli. Mrs. Savella Stechishin, the greatest authority on Ukrainian cooking in North America, frankly equates varenyky with pyrohy in her book "Traditional Ukrainian Cookery." Thus one reads "To reheat Varenyky (Pyrohy)" or "Cheese Dough for Varenyky (Pyrohy)." Others less learned than Mrs. Stechishin claim that varenyky are bigger and fatter than pyrohy. Perhaps it depends on what part of the Ukraine your grandparents came from. Perogy is the name given to pyrohy by Canadians who can't pronounce

Ukrainian properly. Commercially made varenyky, or pyrohy, are always called perogies, so that the ignorant can enjoy them without anxiety over pronunciation.

Bonnie Gerus is a purist. She's a fresh-faced farmer's daughter, with blonde hair and blue eyes, who hates "bought stuff." Although she and her husband, a professor at the University of Winnipeg, live in the city, they use most of their yard for growing vegetables and fruit trees. Bonnie makes her own apple juice, plum jam, and pear preserve, and being Ukrainian, puts up a tremendous amount of cucumber pickles. She freezes the fresh dill that grows in her garden, so that there will be a sprig to put in the borsch in February. All her chickens and eggs come from the family farm. "I can draw forty chickens at a time, nothing to it." She spoke of her grandmother, who jells raspberry juice in a slow oven for hours, and puts a teaspoon of the jellied fruit in her tea instead of sugar, a true Slavic custom.

Bonnie's favorite filling for varenyky is homemade sauerkraut or soured cabbage leaves, which are fermented the same way as sauerkraut, but not shredded beforehand. A few years ago she spent a winter in Moscow, because her husband was studying at the Moscow University. It was getting close to Christmas, when she felt a terrific urge for varenyky made with soured cabbage leaves and sauerkraut. In Manitoba she ate them every year at that time, but no matter where she looked in Moscow, the so-called home of soured cabbage, not a leaf even from the bottom of the barrel could be found. Bonnie began to make her own sauerkraut in the students' dormitory.

Although it was the first time she ever tried it, the sauerkraut was a success. Her husband said, "The smell of good fermenting cabbage hit everyone, as soon as they reached our corridor."

Bonnie's family were part of the huge emigration from the Ukraine to western Canada that occurred between 1896 and 1914. These were the people who farmed the west, who brought dill, poppyseed, buckwheat, spinach, horseradish and the towering sunflower to the prairies. The black soil in Manitoba and Saskatchewan was grain-growing land like that in the Ukraine, the bread-basket of Russia. Over half a million Canadians of Ukrainian descent live all over

Canada now, but most of them have their roots in the prairies. There are place-names like Bukowinia, and a statue of Shevchenko, the nationalist Ukrainian poet, overlooks the Manitoba legislature.

Ukrainian food is based on grain. When Honoré de Balzac visited the Ukraine in the 1840's he noted, "I counted seventy-seven ways of making bread." A Ukrainian answered, "And no one has ever counted all our cakes." Indeed, many Ukrainian cakes are made from finely crushed bread crumbs instead of flour.

Bread is the symbol of prosperity, and a holiday table is never without the traditional kolach, a round, braided egg bread. Every year Toronto has an annual multicultural festival, Caravan, and the Ukrainian pavilions always have a huge twisted kolach at the entrance, greeting the "guests" who pass through their door. The favorite garnish over perogies, vegetables and potatoes is bread crumbs browned in butter.

The fresh water lakes on the prairies supplied good whitefish and pickerel to the early Ukrainian settlers. This is a fine recipe, even for frozen fish.

Pashtet of Fish

a delicious fish soufflé

Cook vegetables and half of fish in salted water until barely tender. Remove the cooked fish and mash it up. Grind or blend the uncooked fish. Mix the cooked and uncooked fish together. Add egg yolks, vegetables, lemon juice, and the rest of the ingredients. Mix well, fold in beaten egg whites. Pour mixture in a well-buttered pan or mold. Place pan in hot water. Bake about 30 to 40 minutes, until center is firm. Ukrainians like to eat this with horseradish or a hot tomato sauce. Excellent cold.

½ cup mixed diced vegetables [onions, carrots, peas, etc.]
1 cup water
1 lb. fish fillets [white-fleshed] [454 g]
1 tbsp. melted butter
3 egg yolks
3 tbsp. cream
3 tbsp. bread crumbs
2 tsp. lemon juice
  salt and pepper
3 egg whites
  fresh chopped dill, or parsley [about two tbsp.]

Holubtsi

Everyone has eaten cabbage rolls or Holubtsi, but not many have tried it with a buckwheat and mushroom filling. Both ingredients are traditionally Ukrainian and delicious. Vegetarians will love this.

Cabbage Leaves

Remove core from a cabbage. Place cabbage in a deep pot and pour boiling water through hollowed core until the cabbage is completely covered with water. Let it sit until leaves are soft and pliable. Drain water and cut off hard center rib from each leaf. The larger leaves may be cut in two. Now they are ready for stuffing.

Buckwheat Filling

2 cups medium buckwheat
   groats
1 egg
½ lb. mushrooms [227 g]
4 tbsp. butter or fat
2 tsp. salt
4 cups boiling water or
   soup stock
10 oz. sour cream [284 ml]
   tomato sauce

Pour groats in large fry pan and add egg. Stir-fry at a medium heat until egg has been absorbed, and the groats smell nut-like and toasted. Add water, fat, salt, and mushrooms. Cover pan, and cook on top of stove or in oven for ½ hour. The water should have disappeared, and each grain of buckwheat should be separate.

Place a generous spoonful of buckwheat mixture on each open cabbage leaf. Roll them up and tuck in the ends. Amateurs use toothpicks to insure that the filling won't escape. Place cabbage rolls side by side in a deep pot and add tomato sauce, sour cream, or a little soup stock to the holubtsi. Cook until you think it's done. Some people like them cooked 2 hours; some people like their cabbage crisp and only cook them for 40 minutes. They may be reheated. Add bacon bits, browned bread crumbs, or smother them with more mushroom just before heating.

As I mentioned before, the bible for Ukrainian cooks in North America is Savella Stechishin's "Traditional Ukrainian Cookery". Mrs. Stechishin grew up on a farm near Krydor, Saskatchewan, and was the first female graduate from the University of Saskatchewan of Ukrainian descent.

As founder of the National Ukrainian Woman's Association, she was in a position to ask for recipes from Ukrainian women in even the most remote districts of Canada. She tried and tested them for years, before the book was published in 1957. "You know," she says, "they never measure; it's always, go to the cold room and cut off a hunk of butter."

Egg Drops for Soup

Savella Stechishin's "Traditional Ukrainian Cookery"

Perfect to add in chicken soup or borsch at the last minute.

Beat egg and then beat in remaining ingredients. Pour slowly from the end of a spoon in a thin stream into a simmering soup and let cook 2 to 3 minutes. If poured from a height, the shape of the drops will be improved, (or put through a sieve).

1 egg
1 tbsp. water
4 tbsp. flour
1/8 tsp. salt

Meatless Borsch

A version of the meatless borsch in "Traditional Ukrainian Cookery"

This soup is usually served at Christmas Eve supper because meat dishes are forbidden. For non-Ukrainians it's an excellent vegetarian soup —especially with the egg drops in it.

Many delicatessens, Chinese, Eastern European, and even health shops carry dried boletus mushrooms or even chanterelles. Their taste is far more distinctive than the fresh variety that is found on every supermarket counter. And the soup benefits. If you can't find any dried, use a cup of fresh mushrooms.

Soak mushrooms in lukewarm water for 30 minutes. Place beets, parsley, onion and peppercorns in water. Cook until beets are barely done. Remove beets and cut into long

½ cup dried mushrooms
1 large onion chopped
2 large beets
1 parsley root scraped and cut in thin strips
4 peppercorns
8 cups water

123

1 carrot cut in thin strips
2 large diced potatoes
1 large stalk celery diced
1 cup of canned tomatoes or tomato juice
3 cups shredded cabbage
  juice of a lemon or vinegar
  salt and pepper

thin slices. Replace sliced beets, add carrot, potato, celery and tomato juice or canned tomatoes. Cook for 10 minutes and then add cabbage. Simmer until cabbage is barely cooked. It should retain some crispness. Add salt, pepper and lemon juice. This borsch should be slightly tart.

Veal Kidneys Braised in Sour Cream Mushrooms and Dill Pickles

2 or 3 veal kidneys
3 tbsp. flour
1 chopped onion
1 stalk celery sliced
1 small carrot, diced
¼ bay leaf
3 tbsp. butter
2 medium dill pickles
1 to 2 cups soup stock
½ lb. sliced mushrooms [227 g]
1 or 2 cloves crushed garlic
½ cup sour cream [or a little more]
  salt and pepper

Remove all fat and membrane from the kidneys. Split them lengthwise and cut away white tubes. Wash. Pat dry. Cut kidneys in thin slices and roll them in the flour. Heat butter in fry pan, add kidneys and onions, brown slightly, and then add celery and carrot. Pour stock over the whole mixture, add remaining ingredients (except sour cream), and include a little juice from the pickle jar. Simmer until vegetables are tender.

Add sour cream at last moment. Serve with rice, noodles or kasha.

124

Roast Pork with Mock Mustard Cream Sauce

Preheat oven to 325° F (165° C). Place fat or oil in casserole, heat until almost smoking; sear pork until brown. Remove pork and most of fat from casserole. Stir in vegetables, garlic, herbs. Cover and cook for 2 hours. When meat is done, remove as much fat as possible from its juices and mash the vegetables into a gravy. Add ½ cup water, wine or stock. Keep warm.

3 lbs. boneless roast of pork [1.36 kg]
4 tbsp. rendered fresh fat or cooking oil
1 onion, sliced
1 carrot, sliced
2 cloves garlic, if desired parsley, ¼ tsp. thyme, bay leaf

Pour the vinegar and peppercorns into a casserole and boil until the vinegar has reduced to about a tablespoon. Pour in the gravy mixture from the roast and boil the sauce down for a couple of minutes.

Add cream, simmer for 5 minutes, adding salt to taste. Beat in cornstarch mixture and simmer 2 or 3 minutes more. Sauce should be quite creamy. Correct seasoning. Add softened butter and remove sauce from stove.

Serve in a gravyboat alongside roast pork. The meat and sauce should serve 6 people.

Mock Mustard Cream Sauce
⅓ cup cider vinegar
10 crushed peppercorns
1 to 2 cups whipping cream
½ tsp. cornstarch mixed with 1 tsp. water
1 to 2 tbsp. softened butter

Sour Cream and Buckwheat Medivnyk (Honey Cake)

an adaptation from Mrs. M. Nowosad

1 cup honey [preferably
   buckwheat honey]
½ cup butter
1 cup brown sugar
4 eggs, separated
3 cups sifted flour
2 tsp. baking soda
1 tsp. baking powder
2 tsp. ginger
1 cup thick sour cream
1 cup chopped walnuts
½ cup raisins

Bring honey to a boil and cool. Cream butter and add sugar. Add egg yolks one at a time and beat until fluffy. Beat in honey. Sift flour and dry ingredients. Add alternately with sour cream to the honey mixture. Stir in nuts and raisins. Beat egg whites stiff and fold into batter. Spoon into buttered tube pan.

Bake at 325° F (165° C) for 50 to 55 minutes. Lower the temperature for the last 15 minutes of baking to 300° F (150° C).

Kasha and Mushrooms

2 cups kasha
1 egg
2 tsp. salt
   about 4 cups boiling water,
   or enough just to cover
   kasha
1 or 2 tbsp. fat if desired
   [butter, chicken fat, or
   drippings]
   mushrooms
   onions

Put the dry kasha in a shallow pan on low heat. Mix in the raw egg and dry the mixture thoroughly over the stove, stirring frequently. The kasha should begin to smell nut-like, but be careful not to scorch it.

Put the kasha in a casserole; add fat, salt and boiling water. Cover and cook at 400° F (205° C) for 15 minutes. Lower the temperature and cook a little longer — until the kernels are separated and fluffy and the water has evaporated. Mix some fried mushrooms and onions with this.

Instead of water, substitute boiling chicken soup or consommé for a richer taste.

Honeyed Nuts

Boil together until mixture is very slightly burnt. Mix thoroughly until nuts are covered with honey. Pour on damp wooden board. Undo in clusters while still hot.

4 tbsp. honey — Manitoba buckwheat honey does very well
1 lb. nuts, preferably almonds [454 g]
1 tbsp. cocoa
2 tbsp. butter

Rose Petal Preserves

To avoid washing the petals, pick them after a good rain. Pick the petals of the fully or partly opened roses, pulling them with one grasp; while holding them in the hand, cut off the yellow tips that have been attached to the crown of the blossom. These yellow ends must be removed because they have a bitter taste. Spread the petals on a clean wire screen to let the stamens and pollen fall through, and then pick the petals over.

Scald with boiling water and drain. As an alternate method, omit the scalding, sprinkle the petals with some sugar and crush with the hand to remove bulkiness. Sprinkle very

generously with lemon juice; otherwise, the petals will turn brown. Use equal quantities of sugar and petals. Use 1 part water for 3 parts rose petals. Combine sugar and water and bring to a boil. Add the petals and simmer, stirring frequently, for about 10 minutes. Add more lemon juice if necessary.

Remove from stove and let the preserves stand overnight. Then bring to a boil once more and cook until syrup is thick and clear. Pack into hot sterilized jars.

Uncooked Rose Petal Preserves

from Mrs. Wolchuk

Follow the directions in the preceding recipe for Rose Petal Preserves but do not scald the petals. Sprinkle the petals with some sugar and lemon juice, and crush them well. Chop small quantities until fine, and mix 1 cup of chopped petal pulp with 2 or more cups of sugar and mash some more in a bowl. It must be as smooth as possible before you seal it.

13. The Bible Group

When I was a young girl in Winnipeg, I had only one ambition. I wanted to cook better than anyone else. I was brought up to believe — the better the cook — the better the person. My mother and father revered a certain Mrs. Birnbaum because she made Turkish Delight Strudel with a thinner, whiter, lighter pastry than anyone else, and she put more Turkish Delight in the middle, too. It was a great coup for my parents when Mrs. Birnbaum volunteered to make my wedding strudel.

At the time of my marriage, Jewish weddings always had to have a sweet table — the tortes, cheesecakes, and dainties were all made by friends of the bride's and possibly the groom's parents. A Jewish wedding without a sweet table (and I believe this still is the case in Winnipeg) was practically against the Judaic Code. And a sweet table without wedding strudel was a disappointment to the guests and bad luck for the bride.

Mrs. Birnbaum's donation of wedding strudel had great moral force. A week before the wedding, my nerve had given out and I wanted to cancel everything; I was eighteen and my mother's kitchen suddenly had more attractions than living in a flat in Oxford with a strange man — albeit my husband. But I never said anything to my parents, because I knew that forty rolls of strudel had already been prepared by Mrs. Birnbaum and were waiting to be sliced in four hundred pieces on my wedding day.

Good cooking and moral goodness were inextricably mixed up in my mind, especially because of my father. He was extremely critical of how women cooked. (If my father knew any man that cooked, he was considered such an aberration that my father became embarrassed.) A housewife was not necessarily worthy, however, just because she could make barley or chicken soup. If she forgot to scoop all the fat off the soup, he called her a danger to his life and limb — a globule of fat could manufacture enough heartburn to spoil his evening. One of my earliest memories is watching my mother bending over a boiling pot, catching up each widening and narrowing circle of fat with a teaspoon and dumping it into a slops bowl. My father knew what good kichel were: dry puffs of egg pastry that disintegrated at the touch of a wet tongue. If the kichel stuck to the roof of his mouth instead of dissolving immediately with the tea, he considered the kichel-maker a fraud — and would say so, to me and my mother. Few women had as much soul and integrity as my mother and Mrs. Birnbaum.

My mother is a good person who cooks constantly and well. Nothing made her happier than rushing home from a tea party at four to release the knob on the pressure cooker. I used to bring my girl friends home from school, and we'd play our favorite game — gazing into the refrigerator.

On the top shelf was a jar of half-opened dill pickles, brought up from the basement, two jars of different soups, flecked by cabbage and barley, eggplant salad, homemade mustard for the pickled brisket on the lower shelf, Aunty Dolly's chopped herring, and Jewish antipasto. Jewish antipasto was tuna fish, olives, cauliflower, little onions, and green pepper pickled in a brine for three weeks and eaten on a lettuce leaf.

Covered casserole dishes occupied the middle shelf — sweet and sour meatballs (always a side dish, never a main course), a low pan of meat blintzes, and an oval dish with chicken livers and fried onions, rendered chicken cracklings and "eggies." Eggies were what my brother and I called the unborn eggs, (the whites and shell were not yet formed), that came from the inside of the hen mother bought from the kosher butcher. She'd boil them in the soup and mix the eggies with the livers, onions and cracklings. There was a Pyrex dish filled with a noodle pudding of some sort, and a bowl of my grandmother's gefilte fish that my father ate on Thursday nights. My brother and I hated gefilte fish, so my mother would prepare a dish of pickled fresh salmon with lemon, peppercorns, and onion rings, that lay near the gefilte fish.

Little wax paper squares hid leftovers — a chunk of apricot bundt, a piece of Russian butter cake, left over from a luncheon, and some donations from friends who wanted mother to try their efforts. The donations were never eaten by my father, who mistrusted things with chocolate chips and, God forbid, colored marshmallow. The smoked fish, goldeye and coonie were wrapped up and placed on the refrigerator door with the eggs and butter. Four round cookie tins, with a different variety of pastry in each, sat on top of the refrigerator.

A neighbor accused my mother of Overcook. But that neighbor used to serve her children and husband Kraft Dinner and sandwiches for **dinner**. We were only four in the family, but you never knew who might drop in. Besides, my mother had to cook for Auntie Zora. Auntie Zora was the one sister in her family who hated cooking. When Zora made canned tomato soup it was always full of lumps because she thought stirring soup was boring. There would always be a platter in the refrigerator with a little warning sign stuck on with a toothpick "Children Do Not Touch, This is Zora's Stuffed Chicken."

My mother belonged (and still does) to a Bible group. Twelve or fourteen of her friends gathered together every two weeks to study the Bible in depth, guided by a teacher or a friend who had a Ph.D. The Bible Group meetings would take place at a different house around lunch hour; naturally it was the duty of each lady whose turn it was to entertain to provide something to eat. I believe the phrase was "a dessert luncheon" which meant you could serve a main course as well as a dessert for lunch, but you couldn't get away with serving lunch without dessert. All the ladies were good cooks, and the fact they were studying the Bible increased my feeling that good cooks had better souls than other women.

Twenty years later, when someone mentions Joseph and his Brothers, I see Cheese Pies, Poppy Seed Cookies, Bundts, and Apple Fluden spread out on his rainbow coat. If a lady missed a session, she'd call up my mother and ask her what the discussion was about. My mother would try and give an intelligent resumé of the hidden meaning behind the Story of Esther or whatever, but she really fell into her stride when the inevitable question "What was the baking like" was finally broached.

Blintzes

Dough

3 eggs
1½ cups water
1 cup flour
a little salt

Filling

1 lb. dry cottage cheese [454 g]
a bit of sugar [a couple of tbsp. if you like a sweeter filling]
2 eggs
melted butter

Beat eggs, and add water and salt; stir in sifted flour, beating until smooth. Slightly grease a hot 8″ (20.3 cm) frying pan. Pour in just enough batter to make a thin sheet. Cook only one side of blintz until firm enough to turn, baked side out, on a pastry board.

Many Jewish people were raised to the sound of grandmothers banging out the blintz skin. This was done by rapping the overturned frying pan on a pastry board. You can keep two frying pans going at the same time; while one is being rapped, the other cooks.

Notice that water, not milk, is used. It makes for a thinner blintz dough. Thick blintz doughs are crass.

Mix it all up. Place 1 tbsp. cheese filling on one end of the blintz skin and roll, folding in the ends. Very gently cook the blintzes in a buttered skillet until they look a little brown — but not too. Serve hot with sour cream and strawberry jam. You can make the blintz skins in advance and brown them later in the oven, or on top of the stove.

Russian Butter Cake

Cream butter and sugar well; add egg. Add the flour and baking soda; mix well and divide the dough into 5 portions. Pat out dough into 8 inch (20.3 cm) layer-cake tins. If you have only two, you will need to bake the dough in stages. The best pans are those with a little lever attached to help remove the baked dough. Otherwise use foilwrap to line the pan.

Bake the dough for about 10 minutes in a 375° F (190° C) oven. Remove the layer from the pan after it has completely cooled. It will be very brittle, so handle carefully. Continue until you have 5 baked layers.

You may substitute ½ cup of rum for ½ cup of the milk. But put it in towards the end of the cooking.

Mix egg yolks, sugar, cocoa, cornstarch and milk. Put into double boiler and cook until thick. Add vanilla and 1 tsp. butter. Spread filling in between layers. Ice with chocolate icing of your own choice. Put into refrigerator for at least 48 hours. It must be very moist. Cake should be removed from refrigerator 3 hours before serving, to soften.

1 cup butter
1 cup white sugar
1 egg
2 cups bread flour, sifted
¼ tsp. baking soda

Filling
½ cup sugar
1 tbsp. cornstarch
2 cups milk
2 tbsp. cocoa
2 egg yolks
1 tsp. vanilla
1 tsp. butter

Jewish Antipasto *Very good with drinks*

2 large carrots
2 large celery stalks
1 small cauliflower
1 tin green stuffed olives
3 tins tuna fish with oil
1½ bottles of chili sauce [11 oz. size] [313 ml]
½ bottle ketchup
2 tsp. Worcestershire sauce
juice of a lemon
½ lb. mushrooms [preferably fresh] [227 g]
1 bottle pickled small onions
1 to 2 tsp. horseradish

Parboil carrots, celery, cauliflower just until they are barely soft. Slice in chunks. Mix together with sauces and rest of ingredients. Bottle. May be kept in fridge for several weeks.

My Mother's Pickled Salmon

4 or 5 lb. salmon [with the head] [2.27 kg]
1 cup wine vinegar
1 tbsp. sugar
salt and pepper to taste
3 large sliced onions
½ cup water
2 tbsp. pickling spice wrapped in a little cheese-cloth [make sure there is only 1 dried red pepper among the spices]
lemon slices

To be eaten cold, with challah or egg bread. If you can't find a salmon, whitefish will do.

Bring vinegar, sugar, water, onion and pickling spices to a boil and taste the liquid to make sure the sweet-sour combination is to your liking. Place fish in water, making sure the liquid barely covers the fish. Take out pickling spice. Cook fish at a simmer for 20 minutes, or until the flesh flakes. Five minutes before you finish cooking the fish, throw in some lemon slices. Remove the fish and stock from the stove and let the fish cool in the liquid. Remove the head. The liquid should jell slightly. This is delicious on a hot summer day. The head provides the gelatine which jells the liquid.

134

Gefilte Fish as Mother Makes It

with Lake Winnipeg fish

Sauté onion until it is soft, but not brown. Chop even more finely and mix onion, fish, eggs, water, bread, sugar, salt, pepper together with an electric mixer. The fish-bread-egg mixture must be very fine. Pat into oval balls.

Slice up several carrots, onions, and celery and put them in a large pot. Cover the vegetables with water and season with salt, pepper, and a tbsp. of sugar. Bring water to a boil and drop fish balls carefully into simmering water. Cook at a slow temperature on top of stove for 2½ hours.

Serve hot with vegetables and broth. Or serve cold with horseradish and sliced tomatoes.

3 lbs. ground whitefish and pickerel [1.36 kg]
1 large onion, sliced finely
3 whole eggs
  a full tbsp. salt
2 tsp. ground black pepper
1 tbsp. sugar
1½ cups water
2 slices white bread, squeezed through with water, and finely crumbled
  additional sugar, salt and pepper

Auntie Dolly's Chopped Herring

Eat with crackers or bread before the main course.

Soak herring in cold water overnight. Put cut-up fish, eggs, crumbled bread, apple through a food grinder. Season with salt, pepper or sugar if needed. May be kept in refrigerator for several weeks.

2 large fat herring [these may be found in a barrel of brine at Jewish delicatessens]
2 large boiled eggs
1 green apple, chopped
1 thick slice of pumpernickel bread, soaked in a little vinegar
1 Spanish onion, chopped

Pickled Brisket

Brisket is a cut of meat that is very popular with Jewish people. According to dietary law, no portion of an animal may be eaten if it is taken from the hind quarters. The brisket is above the hind quarters.

1 boned brisket, from 5 to 7 lbs. [2.27 kg to 3.17 kg.] Rub a scant cup of coarse salt into the meat.
Make a brine with:
½ cup brown sugar
1 tsp. saltpeter
2 cloves garlic chopped
    a handful of pickling spices
4 or 5 dried chilis
½ cup lukewarm water

Pour brine over meat, and cover with a little cold water. Leave in fridge for 10 days, and turn occasionally.

Wash off spices and brine in cold water. Place meat in a large uncovered roaster, and place chopped onions over and under it. Rub a little vegetable oil and mustard on top of brisket. Roast for 4 to 5 hours in a low oven, about 300° F (150° C), until meat is tender. May be eaten hot or cold.

Bible Luncheon Cheese Pie
Rich and Special
but not a dessert. It is eaten as a main course.

Combine as for pie crust.

Crust
½ cup butter
½ cup Crisco
2 cups flour

Roll out crust, leaving ¼ of it for top. Place crust in a Pyrex pie plate. Add filling. Place lattice strips of crust on top. Bake in 375° F (190° C) oven for ½ hour, or until crust is crisp but not brown.

2	tsp. baking powder
2	eggs
¼	cup milk
	salt

Eat hot with sour cream and strawberries. This may be reheated, but tastes better the first time round.

Filling

1½	lbs. cottage cheese [½ lb. creamed 226 g, 1 lb. dry 454 g]
2	eggs
¼	cup sugar
	juice ½ lemon
¼	cup melted butter

Apricot Bundt Cake

**A fine-textured cake that may be eaten without a fork.
Good for large buffet parties.**

Let dried fruit stand in hot water until it is softened. Drain well and chop. Sift flour, baking powder and salt. Cream butter, add sugar, eggs and vanilla. Add flour and milk alternately, starting and ending with flour. Fold in apricots. Mix cinnamon, flour (1 tbsp.) and brown sugar together. Pour ⅓ of the batter in a well greased bundt pan or heavy mold. Add ⅓ cinnamon mixture, then ⅓ batter, then the cinnamon mixture, then batter. Add rest of cinnamon. Bake at 350° F (175° C) for 1 hour.

Unmold when cool.

1½	cups dried apricots
3	cups flour
2	tsp. baking powder
½	tsp. salt
1	cup butter or shortening
1	cup sugar
3	eggs
1	tsp. vanilla
1	cup milk
⅔	cup brown sugar
1	tbsp. flour
1	tbsp. cinnamon
4 to 6	tbsp. melted butter

14. Masala, Methi, and Urad Dal

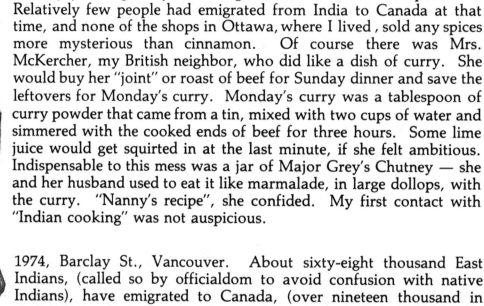

Twenty years ago, my knowledge of Indian cuisine was primitive. Relatively few people had emigrated from India to Canada at that time, and none of the shops in Ottawa, where I lived, sold any spices more mysterious than cinnamon. Of course there was Mrs. McKercher, my British neighbor, who did like a dish of curry. She would buy her "joint" or roast of beef for Sunday dinner and save the leftovers for Monday's curry. Monday's curry was a tablespoon of curry powder that came from a tin, mixed with two cups of water and simmered with the cooked ends of beef for three hours. Some lime juice would get squirted in at the last minute, if she felt ambitious. Indispensable to this mess was a jar of Major Grey's Chutney — she and her husband used to eat it like marmalade, in large dollops, with the curry. "Nanny's recipe", she confided. My first contact with "Indian cooking" was not auspicious.

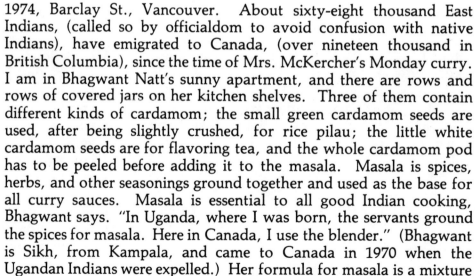

1974, Barclay St., Vancouver. About sixty-eight thousand East Indians, (called so by officialdom to avoid confusion with native Indians), have emigrated to Canada, (over nineteen thousand in British Columbia), since the time of Mrs. McKercher's Monday curry. I am in Bhagwant Natt's sunny apartment, and there are rows and rows of covered jars on her kitchen shelves. Three of them contain different kinds of cardamom; the small green cardamom seeds are used, after being slightly crushed, for rice pilau; the little white cardamom seeds are for flavoring tea, and the whole cardamom pod has to be peeled before adding it to the masala. Masala is spices, herbs, and other seasonings ground together and used as the base for all curry sauces. Masala is essential to all good Indian cooking, Bhagwant says. "In Uganda, where I was born, the servants ground the spices for masala. Here in Canada, I use the blender." (Bhagwant is Sikh, from Kampala, and came to Canada in 1970 when the Ugandan Indians were expelled.) Her formula for masala is a mixture

of peppercorns, whole cloves, cinnamon bark, cardamom, whole cumin and celery seeds. There is no single recipe for masala; every sect, every region of India has its favorite blend — the proportions depend on individual taste.

Looking, or rather spying, further in Bhagwant's pantry I discovered pistachios, cashews for her rice dishes; yellow turmeric which adds flavor and color to curry; saffron threads an essential but expensive spice, (it comes from the stigmas of crocuses), anardama, or dried pomegranate seeds; methi, or fenugreek seed; urad dal, a small bean; whole mustard and coriander seeds, and dried chili peppers. Nowhere on her shelves did I find a blue can of something marked "curry powder." Bhagwant has never heard of Major Grey's chutney, either. She makes her own "pickle" as she calls it — a tart preserve made from carrots, or lemons, or peppers, depending on what is cheap and plentiful at the time. When I opened her refrigerator, I found another mixture that she makes in quantities, also kept in a sealed jar: garlic, fresh ginger, salt and lemon juice, crushed in the blender, and used for meat or fish curry.

True Indian cuisine, then, needs far more subtle ingredients than Mrs. McKercher's curry, but the spices and herbs are not difficult to find, these days. There are shops selling all the spices on Bhagwant's shelf in every major city in Canada. In Ottawa, where the East Indian and Pakistani population is not as large as in Toronto and Vancouver, at least three major fruit shops in the Ottawa Market carry everything mentioned. Unflavored yoghurt is another essential; it acts as a cooling contrast to the spicier dishes. Once you have all these things the actual cooking is not too complicated.

Bhagwant works full-time as a claims adjuster for the British Columbia government, "we look after bashed cars", and finds cooking a curry or a pilau a relaxing avocation. She is a highly organized woman, with precise movements and deft hands; her knife never slipped, nor did the frying oil splatter, as she prepared a feast for thirteen of her friends. She made everything herself, from the chapati, (a flat whole-wheat bread fried in a pan), to the yoghurt. For the yoghurt, she simmers milk and leaves it overnight in the oven, at a low heat, until it thickens. We ate chicken tika, gulab jamon (deep fried balls, milk powder, soaked in a cardamom sugar syrup, that is not eaten as dessert but before everything else), fish kebabs, a spicy patty made with steamed fresh cod and potato; curried chicken; her rice pilau, and Bhagwant's homemade chutney and yoghurt.

Most Indians I have met drink little or no alcohol, because of religious beliefs, or habit. Bhagwant kept urging me to have a drink. But I noticed that neither she nor her guests were drinking, despite protests that her religious principles were not strong enough to prevent her from taking a glass, every so often. She even produced an almost full bottle of Johnny Walker, with only a half a jigger of Scotch missing. Her guests, who were all East Indian, refused politely, although most admitted to an occasional drink. I asked her when she bought the Scotch. "Oh!" she said, "My brother-in-law gave it to me two years ago, and some has disappeared already." I drank Coca-Cola, along with everyone else.

Masala

Here is a version of Bhagwant's masala, a prerequisite of all Indian cuisine. This is a garam or dry masala.

Pre-heat oven to 200° F [93° C]

For about 2 cups:

1 cup whole cardamom seeds
½ cup whole cloves
½ cup whole peppercorns
½ cup celery seeds
4 3" pieces cinnamon bark
   [7.5 cm]
½ cup whole cumin seeds

If your blender becomes overheated from grinding the spices, add lemon juice, coconut milk, or vinegar for a wet masala. The wet masala will not last as long but is equally authentic. Southern Indians like the wet masala for their rice dishes and the sauces that go with them.

Spread all the seeds out on a flat pan and place in oven. Bake for 25 minutes, making sure the seeds don't brown. Break up cinnamon bark into small pieces that will be easily crushed by the blender. Mix everything together and blend, about a cup at a time, in the electric blender. Store in a tightly sealed jar; the full flavor will last about 5 or 6 months. It is not essential to toast the spices but it does bring out their flavor.

Bhagwant Natt's Chicken Tika

This is easy to make, once you have all your spices, masala, and ground garlic and ginger mixture. When the chicken is cooked, there should be only enough sauce to give it a pungent flavor, not to drown the bird. If you like a spicier chicken, add more masala and garlic and ginger. These measurements are according to Bhagwant's taste; she likes the dish fairly mild.

Mix everything together in a bowl, and pour over chicken. Bake for one hour at a 400° F (205° C) oven. Stir sauce over chicken occasionally, scraping bottom of pan for all the bits. Add a little extra tomato or yoghurt if you feel it's getting too dry.

The pilau and the chicken should be accompanied with different pickles or chutneys, yoghurt, and chapati. Bhagwant mixes her yoghurt with fresh vegetables (chopped), and a small amount of spice.

Serves 4 to 6

6 chicken quarters
½ to 1 cup unflavored yoghurt
1 fresh chopped tomato
½ tsp. chili, dried or powdered
1 tsp. masala
1 tsp. cumin
   pomegranate seeds
1 tbsp. turmeric
2 tbsp. fresh parsley
1 tbsp. fresh garlic-ginger
   mixture
1 tbsp. tomato paste

Yoghurt or Raita with Chopped Parsley, or Mint, Tomatoes & Cucumber

1 cucumber, chopped and drained of all juice

5 tbsp. mint, parsley or cilantro

1 small tomato chopped

1⅓ cup unflavored yoghurt

1 tbsp. of masala heated in an ungreased pan for a minute salt, unsweetened coconut and finely chopped onions may also be added.

Combine all and chill.

Rice Pilau with Pistachios or Cashews & Coconut

2 cups of rice [Indian or basumati rice is preferable; it has a nut-like flavor]

2 tsp. salt
about 2 dozen unsalted pistachios, or cashews or almonds

1 tbsp. fresh ginger root or the ginger garlic mixture.

1 tsp. cinnamon

1 tsp. mustard seeds

4 whole cloves

A memorable rice dish. The secret: spices and masala go into the pan before the rice. It was impossible to get exact amounts from Bhagwant. She just throws in whatever is handy, but it tastes wonderful.

Bring 4 cups of water to a boil in a 3 quart (3.41 l) saucepan. Pour in rice, a little at a time. Add salt and cook for 10 minutes. Strain rice and set aside.

Heat the oil in a 4 quart (4.55 l) cast iron pot until

142

a drop of water will splutter in it. Add cloves, mustard seed, chili, nuts, stirring all the while. Add rice, lime juice, water, saffron and coconut, and grated ginger and garlic. Bring everything to a boil on top of stove, cover rice, and place in 250° F (120° C) oven. Let it cook for 25 minutes or until rice is tender. Extra spicing can be added at anytime.

1 tbsp. of finely chopped fresh or dried chilis
¼ tsp. saffron [or turmeric if you can't bear the price of saffron]
¼ cup coconut
   lime juice
4 cups water
¼ cup cooking oil

Ginger Mint Chutney

This is a wonderful way to use up your left-over garden mint, and makes a good accompaniment to curry.

Combine water, vinegar, lemon juice with 1 cup of mint, ¼ cup of raisins and 2 cloves of garlic. Buzz in blender for about 1 minute. Add rest of mint, raisins, ginger root and garlic. Buzz some more. Keep scraping the sides and add a little more liquid if necessary. Add salt. This may be kept in the refrigerator for some time, in a sealed jar.

2 cups fresh mint leaves, tightly packed
¼ cup vinegar
½ cup scraped, coarsely chopped fresh ginger root
½ cup raisins
4 cloves garlic
½ cup lemon juice
2 tbsp. water
1 tsp. salt

Lamb Curry Indian dinner in a dish

6 large onions sliced
  vegetable oil
2 or 3 cloves crushed garlic
2 tbsp. masala
2 lbs. boned cubed lamb,
  shoulder or loin [907 g]
3 inch piece fresh ginger root
  [7.5 cm], peeled and cut in
  slivers
6 cups water
4 potatoes, peeled and diced
5 large green or red peppers
¼ cup unsalted toasted cashew
  nuts

Sauté onions in oil until golden. Stir in masala, garlic. Add lamb and stir for 10 minutes. Add water and ginger. Cook for one hour, or until meat is tender. Add potatoes and cook for 15 more minutes. Add pepper and nuts and cook for another 5 minutes. Correct seasoning if necessary.

Spiced Mixed Vegetables with Coconut

1 onion, chopped
2 tbsp. masala
1 inch piece fresh ginger root,
  scraped and crushed
  [2.54 cm]
½ tsp. turmeric
¼ cup vegetable oil
2 cloves garlic crushed
1 cup water
1 large carrot, scraped and cut
  into rounds
½ a small cauliflower, cut into
  pieces

Fry onion, masala, ginger, and turmeric in oil, add crushed garlic. Stir until onions are soft. Add 1 cup water, stir in carrot, cauliflower, string beans. Coat everything thoroughly with masala. Stir in coconut, chili pepper and sweet pepper. Salt to taste. Bring mixture to a boil over high heat. Reduce heat to lowest possible point, cover well and simmer for 15 minutes or until vegetables are tender. Check to make sure mixture does not dry out. Add more water if necessary. Just before vegetables are done, add green onions, and chopped Italian parsley. Serve hot with rice.

¼ lb. fresh green beans cut in half [113 g]
1 cup coconut [the unsweetened variety that can be purchased at Indian groceries]
1 fresh hot chili pepper, seeded and chopped
2 red or green peppers, chopped and seeded
salt to taste
green onions, cut into 2 inch lengths [5 cm]
3 tbsp. chopped Italian parsley or coriander [cilantro]

Other vegetables may be substituted, and more coconut added

Naan (An Indian Flat Bread)

Sift dry ingredients. Make a well in center, add beaten egg, and yoghurt. Work in flour mixture, and add just enough milk to make a soft dough. Turn dough on lightly floured board and knead until pliable. Cover dough with towel, and let it stand for several hours.

Put 2 large ungreased cookie sheets in oven and set temperature at 450° F (230° C). Divide dough in 4 or 5 parts. With the palms of your hands pull and flatten dough until it is about 8 inches (20.3 cm) long and 4 inches (10 cm) wide. Lay two naans on each cookie sheet and bake them for 7 to 10 minutes. If they are not brown enough, broil them for 1 minute.

2½ cups flour
2 tsp. baking powder
½ tsp. salt
1/8 tsp. baking soda
1 egg
½ cup yoghurt
6 tbsp. milk

Indian Salad

1 cup thinly sliced Spanish onions
3 tomatoes, peeled, seeded and diced
2 green peppers, chopped
½ cup chopped fresh coriander, or parsley
juice of one lemon
1 tsp. freshly grated ginger root
½ tsp. sugar
2 tbsp. vegetable oil

Mix together, well.

Baked Spiced Whole Whitefish or Pickerel

4 lb. firm-fleshed fish [whitefish, pickerel, flounder] [1.81 kg]
2 tbsp. vegetable oil
1 tsp. salt

½ cup vegetable oil
2 cups finely chopped onions
1 tsp. masala

Sprinkle salt over fish. Pre-heat oven to 400° F (205° C). With pastry brush, spread oil evenly over bottom and sides of a shallow baking dish, large enough to hold the fish. Set aside.

Heat ½ cup of vegetable oil in fry pan, add onions and masala, turmeric and chili, ginger root, lemon juice, coriander, garlic, jaggery or molasses. Cook until mixture is thick, about 10 minutes. Stir in tomatoes and remove from heat.

146

Coat the outside, underside and cavity of fish with this mixture. The greatest proportion of the mixture should go inside the cavity. Cover with foil or well-fitting lid and bake for 25 minutes, or until fish is done. Sprinkle chopped green onion over fish and serve at once with rice.

1 tsp. turmeric
1 tsp. salt
2 tbsp. finely chopped garlic
2 dried hot chilies, washed and seeded
2 inch cube fresh ginger root, scraped and chopped [5 cm]
½ cup lemon juice
3 tbsp. chopped Italian parsley or coriander
1 tsp. Indian jaggery, or molasses
1 cup fresh tomatoes chopped
6 green onions chopped

15. Tiger's Testicles

On Pender Street in Vancouver there is a herbal store that has a dried gila monster displayed in the window: $4.95. Close by lie some tiger's testicles (dried up) with a sign, "restores sexual organ, soak in whiskey first." Presumably it's the tiger's testicles that have to be immersed. Next to the herbal shop is the Bank of Montreal, Chinese style, with a tiled roof curved in the shape of a pagoda and two huge dragons glowering from the eaves. Omens of good luck for Pender Street bankers? Most of the people on the street are Chinese. An old woman passes by, wearing a wide straw hat, like a coolie, and funny cloth shoes with black tips, very Oriental. She walks by a cluster of lounging, long-haired Chinese boys in jeans, who take no notice.

Pender Street is the heart of Chinatown in Vancouver. The Chinese are among the earliest and latest immigrants to British Columbia, where the greatest number of Canadian Chinese live. They first came in the 1860's to pan for gold in the Fraser River. Later the C P R used Chinese coolies for laying track, and the fishing industry at the turn of the century depended heavily upon their labor. Most came from Kwangtung, where, according to Chinese lore, the natives are mad for gambling. When Ciang Chi-Choa, a sort of roving Chinese reporter, visited British Columbia in 1903, he discovered Fan Tan Alley in Victoria and estimated that the Chinese in British Columbia gambled over a million dollars a year.

After 1923, the Canadian immigration laws tightened, and Chinese men were not allowed to bring in their wives or families. The sight of elderly men trudging a lonely path through the Chinatowns of Canada became a familiar one. It was not until 1949 that the Chinese were allowed to vote provincially, or enter the law or medical faculties of the University of British Columbia. Despite injustice and prejudice, the Chinese prospered and added greatly to every aspect of life in the province.

Today, many Chinese who emigrate to Canada come as professional businessmen rather than laborers. They lived a good life in Hong

Kong or other parts of Asia and loved to go to restaurants serving foods from every region of China. Steamed dumplings (dim sum), noodles, light and fluffy chicken velvet, are from the north; sweet and sour fish is from the Yellow River in Honan, and twice-fried chicken with walnuts and hot peppers is a specialty of the inland region of Szechwan, famous for its peppers. Our new Chinese seek similar standards in Canada. The black night of warmed-over chicken-fried rice and mushy chop suey seems to be disappearing, and the new dawn of Peking duck and winter melon (a kind of squash) soup might well be upon us. Not that either dish is a novelty to lovers of Chinese food, but they have begun to appear on menus in this country just in the last few years.

Harvey Lowe, born in Victoria, B.C. over fifty years ago, educated in Shanghai, and yo-yo champion of the world, (London title 1932), "often challenged but never beaten," bridges the gap between the early Canadian Chinese settlers and the new people coming in from Hong Kong. Harvey learned to speak the different Chinese dialects in Shanghai and acts as an interpreter for the CPR immigration services. He also is the manager of the Asia Garden restaurant, which caters mainly to the "smart crowd from Hong Kong." They come in the late evening for dim sum, won ton, and noodles, and Harvey has to keep three Hong Kong chefs in the dumpling section alone. Another section of the kitchen is just for frying. Harvey bought his Hong Kong chefs Canadian-style deep-fat friers, but they ignore those and drop their shrimp balls in old-fashioned woks on hot fire stoves. One man spends his time splitting and deveining fresh shrimps; cold water runs constantly over the semi-cooked vegetables to keep their color and crispness. "Just like in the Hong Kong restaurants," Harvey says.

Harvey is thinking of opening a Russian-style restaurant right in Chinatown, using Hong Kong chefs to make borsch and shashlik, and a Russian orchestra with balalaikas and mandolins to serenade the guests. How fitting this will be for Pender Street I'm not sure, but Harvey Lowe, who's never been beaten in loop-the-loop on two continents since 1932 and plays mah jong until 2 a.m. almost every night, is not a man to be pigeon-holed.

Cloud Ears and Loblaws

Joan Wong is a new immigrant from Hong Kong, who lives in Toronto. Although I had never met her, she promised over the phone to prepare an eight-dish Chinese meal in her home. "It's not difficult," she said, "if you know what you're doing." Everything comes from Loblaws, except the cloud ears. Joan's meal was certainly authentic, but that old lady walking down Pender Street in the coolie hat is light-years as well as thousands of miles away from Joan and her family in Willowdale.

When I rang the doorbell, Joan's daughters, wearing blue jeans and T-shirts with "oh Shit" etched across the chest, led me to the kitchen. A slim girl, her hair styled à la Sassoon, wearing a pants suit that might have been cut by Ungaro, was stir-frying shrimps, scallops and peppers in a wok. "I'm Joan," she said, "have a drink, and that's my husband in the corner, deep-frying Hong Kong milk" (little squares of sweet custard). Monica, Joan's neighbor, who is not Chinese, was washing up some pots and pans.

Joan's husband is a businessman who is often away from home, and Joan works as a medical receptionist in Monica's husband's office. Joan never cooked before she came to Toronto, fifteen months before. In Hong Kong, there were a multitude of restaurants and servants and a mother-in-law who loved to cook. But here, Joan learned to prepare food with great flair — and not only Chinese; she became interested in Hungarian cooking and found someone to teach her how to make tortes and goulash soup.

New Years, she gave a Mongolian fire-pot party for sixty people. A Mongolian fire-pot is an odd looking vessel pierced in the middle with a metal chimney, the base of which is filled with a chicken broth. Uncooked foods like beef, chicken, dried squid, Chinese cabbage (bok choy) are assembled around the hot pot. The guest dips his choice in the simmering pot with chopsticks, and satisfies his appetite and fortifies the broth at the same time.

Besides working and cooking, Joan swims eighty laps a day in her swimming pool; before she married she won the swimming championship of all China. Dogs are her passion; she owns six, which are kept in separate rooms because they fight.

Poodles, short-haired terriers, chows, swimming practice and full-time job notwithstanding, we sat down to a superbly cooked eight-course meal. Like many good cooks Joan never measures and always improvises. "And," she says, "I never use monosodium glutamate."

We ate

Stir-fry scallops and shrimp balls with red and green peppers and cloud ears

Pork shoulder, marinated in ginger, garlic [specialty of her mother-in-law, who is from Fukien]

"Milk" made with coconut milk and eggs, deep-fried

Hot and Sour Soup from Szechwan

Cucumber and dried scallops stew

Stuffed Chinese mushrooms

Noodles with crab and chicken

Chicken cooked with scallops and soy sauce and oyster sauce

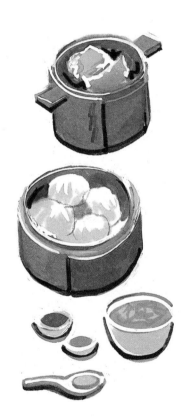

There was no rice on the table. We all ate with chopsticks, except Monica, who faltered in the middle of the meal and was given a fork and knife.

151

After dinner we drank narcissus tea. Narcissus tea is often used for medicinal purposes and is at least two years old. It cost twenty dollars a pound. Joan says that jasmine tea, the kind that is served in Chinese restaurants in Canada, is mundane. "Narcissus tea has no smell of cheap jasmine. True connoisseurs of tea, in Hong Kong, will pay as much as one hundred dollars a pound for what they want."

Stir-Fry Shrimps, Scallops, & Red and Green Peppers with Cloud Ears

2 tbsp. corn or vegetable oil
1 onion, coarsely chopped
1 green pepper coarsely chopped
1 red pepper coarsely chopped
½ lb. medium-sized shrimp [227 g]
½ lb. scallops [227 g]
2 tsp. cornstarch
1 egg white
1 tbsp. dry sherry
1 tsp. soy sauce
  several cloud ears [dried black fungus which looks a bit like mushrooms and is very nutritious. Soak in a little water before using.]
3 slices fresh ginger root, peeled, about 1 inch in diameter [2.54 cm] and 1/8 inch thick [32 mm]
  some chopped green onions

Combine shrimp, scallops and cornstarch in a large bowl. Coat fish well. Add unbeaten egg white, sherry and soy sauce. Have vegetables chopped and within easy reach. Pour oil in fry pan or wok, let it heat, add ginger and scallions, stir for 30 seconds, remove from pan. Add onion, red and green pepper and cloud ears. Stir-fry until vegetables are half-cooked, about one minute. Remove from pan. Stir-fry scallops and shrimp mixture until barely cooked, and covered with a clear glaze. Mix in peppers, onions, cloud ears, green onions, ginger, cooking just enough to reheat. Serve immediately.

152

Hot and Sour Soup

Slice soaked Chinese mushrooms. Heat a fry pan or wok; when hot add oil, and chicken slices. Stir to separate, and add soy sauce. Add mushrooms, bamboo shoots, chili oil, stir 1 minute. Add chicken broth, vinegar and soy sauce. Pour cornstarch mixture into simmering soup. Let thicken, then take soup off heat. Pour soup in hot tureen, and gradually add beaten eggs in a thin stream. Sprinkle with scallions. Add more vinegar or chili if you wish. (May be kept warm, but not at a boil, in oven.)

4 dried Chinese mushrooms, [soak ½ hour first]
1 tbsp. cooking oil
1/3 lb. chicken, [150 g] raw, cut in narrow strips and soaked in 1 unbeaten egg white
1 tbsp. soy sauce
½ cup canned bamboo shoots
½ tsp. chili oil [optional, may be bought at Chinese grocery, try asking for "ah kee"]
5 cups chicken broth
2 tbsp. wine vinegar
2 tbsp. cornstarch mixed with
4 tbsp. hot water
2 eggs lightly beaten
2 tbsp. chopped scallions

Stuffed Mushrooms

Cover mushrooms with 2 cups of warm water, and soak for ½ hour. Remove and drain mushrooms, saving ¼ cup water. Cut away tough stems. Combine soy sauce, wine, sugar and 1 tsp. of cornstarch in a bowl, and stir well. Add ground pork, shrimp, and water chestnuts, mixing well.

Sprinkle rest of cornstarch over mushrooms with underneath, or stem side up. Fill underside of

20 dried black Chinese mushrooms
1 tbsp. soy sauce
1 tbsp. sherry
½ tsp. sugar
2 tsp. cornstarch
1 tbsp. oil
¼ lb. ground pork [113 g]
¼ lb. finely chopped cooked

shrimp, crab meat, or lobster [113 g]

4 drained canned water chestnuts, finely chopped

2 tbsp. oyster sauce [buy at Chinese grocery]

mushrooms equally with meat and fish mixture. Flatten with your fingers. Heat a wok or fry pan and add oil, arrange mushrooms side by side in a single layer on bottom of pan. Lower heat and brown bottom of mushrooms slightly. Pour ¼ cup of mushroom water over mushrooms, bring to simmer and cover pan. Lower heat, and cook for 15 minutes. Stir in oyster sauce, and cook for 30 seconds more. May be kept warm in oven for ½ hour.

Fried Shrimp with Turnips

An odd combination, but extremely satisfactory if the turnips are cut thin enough.

½ lb. of turnips [about ½ medium orange turnip, or one white turnip] [227 g]

2 ice cubes

1 tsp. vinegar

2 tsp. sugar

1 lb. large shrimp [454 g]

1 egg white lightly beaten

2 tsp. cornstarch

½ tsp. salt
   oil for deep frying

Peel and slice turnips paper thin — a potato peeler will do the trick. Marinate them in ice cubes, vinegar and sugar for 2 hours. Squeeze them dry. While turnips are marinating, mix lightly beaten egg white with cornstarch and combine with shrimps. Refrigerate until turnips have finished marinating.

Drop shrimps in about 2 cups of heated oil. Cook about 1 minute. Drain all fat off shrimps. Sprinkle shrimps with salt and toss them together with the turnips.

Chicken Breasts with Fresh Tomato

This is an easy and delicious dish.

Place the chicken pieces on a flat surface, skinned side down. Cut each piece in squares. Place the pieces in a mixing bowl and add the egg white, cornstarch and some salt. Blend well. Refrigerate about ½ hour.

Heat 2 cups of oil in a large fry pan or wok and add chicken. Cook, stirring about 1 minute, then drain all fat off chicken. (Set a large strainer over a bowl.) Pour all but 2 tbsp. of oil from fry pan and add water chestnuts, tomatoes, ginger, garlic and sugar. Cook for 3 minutes, stirring, and add peas. Add the chicken and cook, stirring, until chicken is heated through. Serve immediately.

2 whole chicken breasts, split in half, skinned and boned
1 egg white, lightly beaten
2 tsp. cornstarch
salt
vegetable oil
3 or 4 tomatoes, cut in quarters
8 water chestnuts, sliced
8 thin slices fresh ginger, peeled
2 cloves of garlic flattened with a Chinese cleaver
3 tsp. sugar
½ cup of defrosted green peas

Pearly Meatballs

Soak rice for 45 minutes in about a quart of water (1.14 l). Drain rice and mix it with the salt.

In a separate bowl, mix pork, ginger, sherry, green onions, sugar, 2 tsp. of soy sauce, cornstarch, and 1 tbsp. of water. Blend the meat well with seasonings. Shape into small balls. Roll the balls in the glutinous rice and place them on an oiled large platter. Cover well.

These pearly balls must be steamed. If you don't have a Chinese steamer, found in most kitchen

6 tbsp. of glutinous rice [may be purchased at a Chinese grocery]
1 level tsp. salt
½ tsp. sugar
¼ lb. minced fat pork [113 g]
¼ lb. minced lean pork [113 g]
oil
2 tsp. soy sauce
1 tbsp. cornstarch
2 tsp. sherry
3 tbsp. finely chopped green

onions
3 tbsp. wine vinegar
mixed with
5 tbsp. soy sauce
1 tsp. finely chopped fresh ginger

shops or Chinese groceries, use this simple method. Take a large pot, set two small heat-proof bowls in it, pour water in till ¾ of the small bowls are covered. Set the oiled platter with pearly balls on top of bowls. Cover large pot tightly and cook on top of stove or in oven 300° F (150° C) for 30 to 45 minutes. Replenish water if necessary.

Braised Shin of Beef
A cold dish, to be served as an hors d'oeuvre

2 lbs. boneless shin of beef [907 g]
40 oz. water [1.14 l]
6 tbsp. soy sauce
2 tbsp. sugar
5 slices fresh ginger root, peeled
1 tbsp. oil
4 cloves garlic
2 long thin hot red peppers, sliced [optional]

Bring meat to boil in water. Skim off scum. Stir in soy, sugar, ginger. Reduce heat to moderate and cook for 2 or 3 hours until tender. Remove meat from pot. There should be about 1 cup of liquid in pot; if there is more, remove cover and reduce liquid until you have one cup. Add oil, garlic and pepper and cook 5 minutes more.

Pour liquid over meat. Let cool, and then refrigerate. When meat is cold, cut in thinnest possible slices and serve with braising liquid.

Ginger Beef with Hot Pepper

4 dried black mushrooms
1 cup chopped green onions
1 tbsp. chopped garlic
1 tbsp. chopped fresh ginger
2 tbsp. chopped fresh red or green hot peppers
2 or more hot dried peppers, chopped
3 tbsp. cooking oil

Place mushrooms in a bowl and cover with boiling water. Let stand 15 minutes, drain, squeezing all moisture out of them and cut off tough stems. Chop mushrooms. Combine mushrooms, scallions, garlic, ginger, and dried and fresh peppers. Heat oil in a pan or wok, add sliced beef. Stir quickly, then add soy, and mushroom and pepper mixture. Add cup of chicken broth, cook 3 minutes. Blend cornstarch with 2 tbsp. of remaining broth and stir until thickened. Add salt to taste and coriander. Mix in with beef and peppers. Serve hot.

(All these measurements are approximate. You may add more or less pepper, scallions, mushrooms, etc.)

1 lb. flank steak, cut thinly [454 g]
2 tbsp. soy sauce
½ cup chopped fresh coriander or parsley
1 cup plus 2 tbsp. chicken broth
1 tbsp. cornstarch
   salt

Drunk Duck

Place duck, breast side up, in a large casserole. Cover with water.

Add ginger and star anise to duck, and simmer duck for 20 minutes. Turn off heat, leave cover on pot and let the duck cool in its broth for 3 hours. Remove duck from broth. Remove star anise and ginger. Refrigerate broth until fat comes to top. Scrape off all fat. With a cleaver, cut off wings, legs and thighs of duck. Chop breast in two pieces and discard backbone. Sprinkle the 8 pieces of duck with salt. Arrange pieces of duck in a shallow enamel dish, large enough to hold them in 1 layer. Combine 1 cup of cooled stock with sherry. Pour over duck. Marinate duck in this for 2 days, keeping it covered. Turn occasionally. When ready to serve, chop duck in 2" chunks, (5 cm) bones and all. Decorate with green onions.

This may be prepared ahead of time and served at room temperature.

4 to 5 lb. duck [2.27 kg]
6 slices of fresh ginger, peeled
2 whole star anise or 16 sections of star anise purchased at a Chinese shop, a licorice-flavored spice like an 8 pointed star
1 cup pale dry sherry
2 tbsp. salt
   green onions

157

Lemon Chicken

4 whole chicken breasts boned and skinned, and chopped in 1 inch crosswise slices [2.54 cm]
2 tbsp. light soy sauce
½ tbsp. sesame seed oil [or peanut or corn oil]
1 tsp. salt
1 tbsp. gin
3 egg whites beaten frothy
1 cup of water-chestnut flour, [available in any Chinese-food specialty shop — use cornstarch here too, if you are not a purist]
¾ cup sugar
½ cup white vinegar
1 cup chicken broth
2 tbsp. cornstarch
2 tbsp. water
3 lemons, juice and finely chopped rind
fresh ginger, peeled and sliced, as much as you like
2 cloves garlic, sliced
½ cup shredded canned pineapple
3 small carrots, cut into thin strips
¼ head iceberg lettuce, shredded
3 green onions, finely cut
½ large green pepper, finely cut

Place chicken in shallow bowl. Combine soy sauce, sesame seed oil, salt and gin; pour over chicken. Let sit for 30 minutes. Drain chicken and throw out marinade. Add chicken pieces to beaten egg white and toss to coat. Place the water-chestnut flour on a plate and coat the chicken with the flour.

Add peanut oil to a frying pan or wok to a depth of about ½ inch (1.25 cm) and heat until it sizzles. Add the chicken a few pieces at a time. Brown on both sides and drain.

Place sugar, vinegar, broth, 2 tbsp. cornstarch mixed with water, lemon juice and rind in a large pot. Bring to a boil, stirring until mixture thickens and becomes clear. Keep drained chicken warm in a 200° F (94° C) oven.

Add vegetables, ginger, garlic and pineapple to hot sauce. Remove from heat and pour over chicken.

Serves 4.

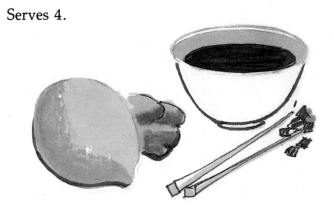

Acknowledgments

You have noticed that this book is as much about people as cooking. My greatest wish, writing Cross Canada Cooking, was to describe how the men and women in this book enrich our country with their different cultures and skills. Interesting as their recipes are, they are not as important as the people themselves.

Each family, every person I met had a new story to tell. Their experiences were as diverse as the geography of Canada. I hope you have enjoyed sharing their experiences as much as I did.

I want to thank from the bottom of my heart right down through my stomach:

Margaret Lyons
Japanese Cooking

Doris Johnson
Icelandic Cooking

Jean Boyd
Scotch Nova Scotia Cooking

Mrs. E. Cholakis
Greek Cooking

Mrs. A. Mikos
Hungarian Cooking

Bhagwant Natt
Indian Cooking

Mrs. H. Zinck
Lunenburg County Cooking

Mrs. Bill Enns
Manitoba Mennonite Cooking

Mme. Alozia Léger
Acadian Cooking

Joan Wong
Harvey Lowe
Chinese Cooking

Mrs. Di Cecco
Italian Cooking

Emmy Lou Allan
Mrs. Pratt
Josephine Davis
Newfoundland Cooking

Savella Stechishin
Bonnie Gerus
Ukrainian Cooking

André Ouellette
French Canadian Cooking

My mother and her Bible Group
Jewish

Index